D1571135

Be Still,
My Soul

A Story of the Seasons
of One's Life

To Sharon,
May you enjoy
the blessings of each
season of life!
Catherine Fetzel Guess.
May 21, 2006.

Be Still,
My Soul

A Story of the Seasons
of One's Life

———

Catherine Ritch Guess

CRM BOOKS
Publishing Hope for Today's Society
Inspirational Books~CDs~Children's Books

Author photograph by Mark Barden.
Front cover photography: Jenn Kullgren McCaughan.
Wedding photography (front flap): Duanne Shinkle-Simon© 2000.
Back cover photography: Norm Cummings,
  The Greater New Milford Spectrum. All rights reserved.
Back cover Pop/ Guess photography: Mario Cardenas.
Kullgren photographs are used by permission.

CRM BOOKS, P.O. Box 2124, Hendersonville, NC 28793
Visit our Web site at www.ciridmus.com

The Reality Fiction name and logo are registered trademarks of CRM BOOKS.

This book is a biographical story of the life of
Harry "Pop" Kullgren. The scenarios
involving Jenn Kullgren McCaughan are a
product of the author's imagination and have been created
as a means of sharing the facts.

Printed in the United States of America
First CRM BOOKS Edition: April 2006
10 9 8 7 6 5 4 3 2 1

10 digit ISBN: 1-933341-11-4
13 digit ISBN: 978-1-933341-11-8
LCCN: 2006921965

In honor of the

102nd Birthday

of

Harry Nils Kullgren
"Pop"

March 5, 2006

Thank You, Jenn

A special word of thanks goes to Jennifer Kullgren McCaughan for so graciously allowing me to take the liberty of using her as the "eyes" of this story. Her real life is exuberant with the energy of a beautiful little girl, Samantha, who lives in a home filled with love, joy and an appreciation of a rich and vibrant heritage. Another word of thanks to her husband, Dave "Lindley," as well, for being so agreeable with my creative liberties of his family. Although parts of your life in this book are fictional, the blessing of an incomparable "Farfar" is not!

May God continue to bless you richly, one day at a time…

    …and to the Kullgren family - Dave and Jean, George and Constance, Christopher, Jonathan, Tom, David, Dave and Jenn McCaughan - Thank you for sharing all your precious letters, photos and memories; to cousin Linnea; to Pop's sister, Nancy Boardy and husband Ulf; and to the Swedish cousins who so willingly assisted with the translations. You are *all* truly blessed to belong to such a wonderful lineage. Thank you for allowing me to be a small part of your family!

~ CR? ~

ACKNOWLEDGMENTS

My deepest gratitude goes to Doug and Debbie Snyder, of Findlay, OH, for introducing me to Pop. Never have I met a more gracious couple. It is their love and respect of others, combined with their charitable spirit, that made this book more than a passing thought. Thank you for your friendship and for the opportunity of a new family!

To Mario Cardenas, executive producer of the CD *This Is My Song*, and his wife, Deb, whose graceful mastery of the flute made my music complete - What a lovely gift you have allowed my son, Jamie Purser, and me to give the world through Pop's music!

To Skitch and Ruth Henderson for allowing me to use their names, and for their acts of kindness and generosity to the community. You've touched many lives in countless ways. And to Jessica Stewart, you're an angel for allowing me the privilege of playing Skitch's infamous Steinway that I'd watched him play for years on *The Tonight Show*. What a dream come true!

To New Milford United Methodist Church and the Education Center, Reverend Stefanie Bennett, Tracie Nixon, Miss Amy and Miss Erin - Your support and encouragement have been priceless.

To Art Carlson and Roberta Buddle, whose welcome and hospitality paved the way for me to be able to write this book and record the CD. For that, and for all the letters and phone calls to Sweden and "wherever" to get answers for me, there are no words to express my thanks. Wouldn't you like to move to warm North Carolina?

To Libby Porter, Rich Tomascak, Ralph Williams and Matthew Guglielmo - You added a special dimension to this book's creation. And Rich, when can I drive the car?

To Kevin O'Neill - New Milford Police Department; Bank Street Coffee House, Mother's on the Green, The Grand Patisserie, The Holiday Restaurant, The Windmill Diner, Clamp's, Wood's Tea Co., and Mary Clancy for being a part of the story.

To Norm Cummings with *The Greater New Milford Spectrum,* and Jenn and Dave McCaughan for the beautiful book and CD cover photography. Your art provides a story in itself.

To Duanne Shinkle-Simon for use of the wedding photograph with Jenn and Pop Kullgren, and to Mario Cardenas for the photograph of Pop and me at the recording session.

Front Cover

(in the bandstand from left to right)
Art Carlson, Harry "Pop" Kullgren,
Libby Porter and Dave Kullgren

(inset)
"Pop"

Front Flap
Pop and Jenn Kullgren McCaughan

Back Cover
The Four Seasons on the Green
Pop and Catherine in recording session

One would think that it is a far distance between
Arvika, Sweden and Stallings, NC, USA. However, as I
began to pen this biographical telling of Harry "Pop"
Kullgren's life, I found that was not the case. That realization first hit me when my son, Jamie, and I went to
practice for the recording of the CD, *This Is My Song*. It
was a couple of days before we were to leave for Connecticut from North Carolina to work with Pop, and we
called Stallings United Methodist Church to see if we
could borrow their sanctuary piano for a couple of hours.
(Jamie and I live 2 hours apart, so my piano was not
available.)

I grew up in Stallings, NC, three doors down from
that church, and although that was not the church my
family attended, I spent a lot of time there in my youth.
Back then, church was community and Stallings was my
community; so in many ways, Stallings UMC *was* my
church. I even played the organ dedication concert there
many years ago. So when Jamie and I were looking for a
church, near his home, where we could practice, that
seemed the logical place to me. It felt like "home."

The Reverend Stephen Pillsbury, minister at

Stallings UMC, welcomed Jamie and I and graciously allowed us the practice time we needed together. He asked about our concert and the CD and when I told him about Pop, I explained, "He sang at some Swedish Methodist Church in New York City, at the corner of Lexington Avenue and... and... and...,"

"Fifty-third Street." Reverend Pillsbury filled in the blank.

"How did you know that?" I asked.

"My father was the minister there at one time."

I couldn't speak and felt that I needed to pick my jaw up off the floor.

Jamie's eyes were wide with astonishment. "Well, there you go, Mom." That's his reply each time we find ourselves in a situation where we know God paved the way for us long before we got there. He turned to Reverend Pillsbury. "This kind of thing happens to my mom all the time all over the world."

From Stallings, Jamie and I went to New York City and as we rode past the United Nations Building, I couldn't help but think of Pop and the years he worked there and what a beautiful story it was that this immigrant came from Sweden, worked diligently and found his way in America to a place where the nations sought for world peace together. It was most fitting.

My favorite memory of meeting Pop is when I looked down at his shoes on the afternoon that we recorded his songs for the CD. They were shoes of a man who had walked many a mile. Not as in literal miles, although he has walked his share, but in figurative miles. They were miles of a man who had experienced everything – at least all the important things – that life had to offer. They were miles that paved the way for a richly meaningful legacy for his family. And they were miles that touched the lives of many people – most recently, Jamie's and mine.

It is my prayer that through *Be Still, My Soul* and *This Is My Song*, you, too, will be touched by this amazing spirit-led man, and that you will come to know, love and appreciate Harry "Pop" Kullgren as I do.

May you discover all the many hidden blessings along the path of your own seasons of life.

CR?

"We lived through it...

we made it through...

one day at a time...

those were the days...

I am blessed...yep..."

"Pop" Kullgren, 101-years-old
November, 2005

Be Still,
My Soul

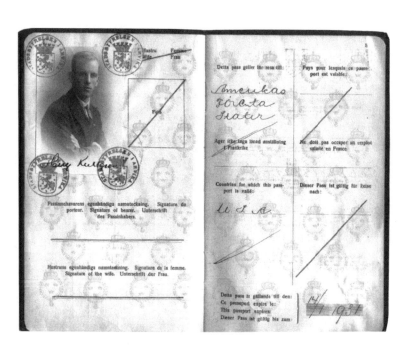

Hustru
Wife
Femme
Frau

Pass

Billy Kellgren (signature)

Passinnehavarens egenhändiga namnteckning. Signature du
porteur. Signature of bearer. Unterschrift
des Passinhabers.

_____

Hustruns egenhändiga namnteckning. Signature de la femme.
Signature of the wife. Unterschrift der Frau.

_____

Detta pass gäller för resa till:

*Amerikas
Förenta
Stater*

Pays pour lesquels ce passeport est valable:

Äger icke taga lönad anställning
i Frankrike

Ne doit pas occuper un emploi
salarié en France

Countries for which this passport is valid:

U. S. A.

Dieser Pass ist gültig für Reise
nach:

Detta pass är gällande till den:
Ce passeport expire le:
This passport expires:
Dieser Pass ist gültig bis zum:

14/ 1931

PROLOGUE

And it came to pass in those days,
    that there were abiding in the same country...
        immigrants...

Lots of immigrants...
    from every country...

Bakers, chefs, stonecutters, brick masons...
    and carpenters...

Carpenters who had followed in their fathers' footsteps...

But there was one particular carpenter who followed in
    the footsteps of his Brother from long ago...

That carpenter's name was Harry Nils Kullgren...
    known to everyone as... "Pop."

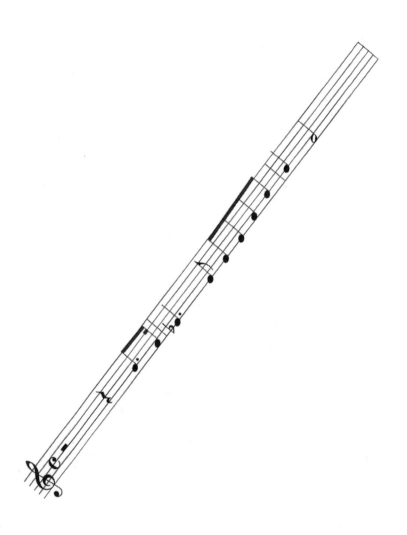

PART ONE

SPRING

New life is evident all around
A time when everything is clean and fresh
and soft and gentle as a baby's breath

The sound of a baby's cry
The tenderness of a youngster's eyes
full of love for everyone he sees

CHAPTER I

Monday

"Have a great day!" came the morning's usual greeting, accompanied by a wave, from the two playschool teachers.

How can they smile day in and day out? Jenn wondered to herself as she dropped Samantha off for a day of fun with her little playmates. *I live for the days I can drop off one two-year-old and they appear to be excited about having an entire roomful.*

The weary mother got in her van and pulled away from the New Milford United Methodist Church parking lot. *But the truth is, I fully do intend to have a great day today. Seven full hours of time alone, the husband's out of town, no screaming child and a day off work. Yes ma'am, Miss Amy and Miss Erin, a great day indeed!*

Jenn McCaughan would have otherwise felt guilty for leaving her precious daughter, Samantha, in day care on her day off. But a house on the market, a "terrible two" who had just hit her new age with full force, and a husband who was out of town for a ten-day photo shoot – on top of her "trying-to-be-the-perfect-mother" lifestyle – had gotten to the point that both her mind and body were screaming for a break.

Isn't that odd? she sneered as she made the left turn back toward the Green of New Milford, Connecticut. *I don't have a screaming child, but I do have a screaming mind and body.*

As if to defend her guilty conscience, she stated aloud, "Samantha has a blast at the Education Center. This is the day that Pastor Bennett comes in and tells the children a Bible story, and Miss Amy and Miss Erin are wonderful teachers. I'm sure she'll have more fun with all her little friends than dealing with my frantic mood today. I'm doing this as much for her benefit as for mine." She popped a CD of relaxing Celtic music into the car's stereo.

The CD had become her particular favorite ever since the past summer's concert of Wood's Tea Co., a band from Vermont who had come to serenade the crowd on the Green. Jenn wasn't sure if it was the wonderful pre-concert patio dinner at Elizabeth's (a fine dining establishment on the corner of the Green) with friends (who also had an approaching two-year-old), the fun of watching two little ones play on a blanket on the lush grass of Connecticut's longest Green or the music of the band. But for whatever reason, the evening had been one that stood out in her mind.

For that same reason, the CD had been played more than any other in her car during the weeks since August when she bought it at the concert. Lindley, as she called her husband since his first name was the same as her dad's and older brother's, had also shown an interest in the group of musicians. That was the reasoning for two other titles by the Wood's Tea Co. carefully hidden in a closet at home until Christmastime.

"Christmastime?" she mouthed softly. *I should probably be taking advantage of this day, like some of the other preschool mothers, to be squirreling away Christmas gifts for my child.* A hefty sigh soon dissuaded any further debate for that idea.

Nope! Today is my day, she confidently determined as she whipped into a parallel parking place on Bank Street.

There had been no definite plans for the day

when Jenn headed out the door that morning. She didn't even have a plan of action when she exited the building at the Education Center. But the van seemed to have a mind of its own as it chauffeured her to the Bank Street Coffee House on New Milford's most affluent street, adjacent to the Green's Main Street.

Ah! What better way to start the morning than to treat myself with a large latte?

Any other day, she would have traipsed across the street to say "Hi" and take a cup of coffee to her mother, Jean Kullgren, who worked at the office of the *New Milford Times*, but her self-made promise of allowing nothing, or no one, to get in the way of her uninterrupted day prevented that.

Another time, she mentally agreed as she opened the coffee house's door and smelled the rich aroma of fresh brew filling the room.

"What can I do for you?" came the enthusiastic offer from a tall, young man behind the counter.

What is it with everyone being so chipper this morning?

Jenn gave him a quick once-over, and figured that he lived at home, took evening classes, had a girlfriend and few responsibilities, as she ordered a Bank Street Crunch, the coffee house's Specialty of the Day. She reached for her money and coffee card, while he went to work adding the flavors and "concocting" her request in a large foam-board cup.

Ah, she sighed, *if the taste of this is any indication as to the rest of the day, it truly is going to be a great day!* A couple of small coffee-flavored ice cubes cooled down the beverage, making it "just right." *I feel just like Goldilocks crouching down into a nice comfy bed, "just right," with my name written on it.*

She slowly sipped the frothy liquid, reminiscent of a candy patty made of pecans and brown sugar, as she pondered over what to do with the rest of her day. A quick glance around the room showed a number of customers reading the local papers. One man sat with a laptop, his fingers typing something apparently of great importance. *Those are things I can do every day. There's got to be something different I can do today.*

Two women at the table behind her began to chat about the current selection of their book club. "I think I'll go out on the Green and read while the children play on the tank," one stated. "It's showing signs of being a perfect fall day."

"About time," replied the other. "That record rainfall of last week and all the flooding in the area surely took a toll on me."

Jenn had been so busy at work, and then packing for the upcoming move, that she hadn't paid much attention to the nine days of constant rain, dropping between 10 -13.5 inches in the area. *Well, there was that detour around the sinkhole on the way to the Bradley International Airport two days ago.*

Then Samantha and I had to take a back way to church yesterday, she suddenly recalled. She'd been so busy rushing out to enjoy her "free" day that she had paid no attention to the shallow standing of water still on Route 7 on her way to drop off Samantha.

Maybe that's another reason I felt so out of control, she reasoned. *Nine days indoors with a two-year-old.* Jenn downed another sip of the delicious latte. *That's enough to drive anyone to insanity!*

"That's a great idea," she heard from behind her. "An hour on the Green would do me a world of good, too. Besides, a good book always rescues me from the drudgeries of life."

"Great! What are we waiting for?"

Jenn heard the chairs behind her scooting across the wooden floor. She turned just in time to see the two women exiting the coffee house and taking a left turn down Bank Street's sidewalk toward the Green.

A book, huh? A rescue from the drudgeries of life, huh? How long has it been since I've taken the time to sit down with a good book? She gave an audible chuckle at her realization. *I read to Samantha every night, but I haven't read a book of my own all the way through since before she was born.*

With that thought, she picked up her latte and walked next door to Baileywick Books. Although she had not been a regular customer since marriage and a new career, she recognized the place immediately like the face of an old friend. Jenn adored small bookstores like this one. There was a cozy feel of the walls filled with books, narrow aisles between rows of shelves, and an aura of mystery created by the dark corners that could not be recreated by the chain stores. This store was perfectly indicative of the "village" dominance still present in New Milford. She took a moment to pause at the front door and become reacquainted with the rows and the arrangement of literary selections.

"Jenn Kullgren!" exclaimed the woman behind the counter. "Oh, I'm so sorry," she hastily added. "I know you're married. It's just that I haven't seen you in so long that your married name has slipped my mind."

"That's quite alright," Jenn smiled. "It happens all the time. McCaughan. It's Jenn McCaughan. People tell me it's hard to get used to a new surname for someone they've known for a long time."

"Correct. I'm also sorry to say this is not the first time I've made that mistake with someone. What can I help you with today? Is that precious little darling of yours in need of a new book? I hear your mother rave about her every time she comes in here."

"No… no, I'm actually looking at something for myself," Jenn sheepishly admitted as she walked toward the new fiction section.

"Good for you! Too many young mothers find themselves so busy with their babies that they neglect their own needs. Reading is a wonderful therapy."

"Yes, so I've heard," Jenn replied as she picked up title after title in search of something appealing.

"Anything particular in mind?"

"No… not at all. I happen to have a day off and I need a break from the constant attention required by a 'terrible two.' Something that can transform me." She reached for still another title.

"Why not an old classic?" suggested a voice from the back of the store. "Some satiric humor by Mark Twain? *A Connecticut Yankee in King's Arthur's Court* is a most transforming tale."

"Hmmm…," paused the contemplative young mother as she walked toward the voice. "I'm not too sure I want to delve that deep into a classic. I was thinking about something much lighter." *Actually you've not thought about too much at all,* Jenn reminded herself, *except having a day alone.*

"You know that Mark Twain lived in Hart-ford?" casually asked the woman who had greeted Jenn.

"Yes... yes, I do know that. My brother, Tom is going there tonight, in fact, for a special presenta-tion by a well-known television personality. One of his best friends, who works at the Mark Twain House and Museum, reserved a ticket for him. Tom took Lindley and I over recently for a tour." She thought back to how much she'd enjoyed that day.

"Mark Twain, huh? A slow barge ride down the Mississippi might be a perfect way to relax."

"Remember, *A Connecticut Yankee in King Arthur's Court* isn't quite the same as Tom Sawyer and Huck Finn," cautioned the woman who had rec-ognized Jenn.

"But it will surely take your mind off all the garbage of the twenty-first century," assured the woman who'd made the suggestion.

"Okay, you've talked me into it. How much damage do I owe you?"

"Leave your damage behind on the Green as you read this book. You owe us $8.58."

Jenn already had the book out of the paper bag and was leafing through the pages by the time she hit the front door.

"Do you really think that book was the best

choice?" questioned the cashier after Jenn was out of earshot.

"Listen, the transformation of Twain's character in that book is nothing compared to the one that young woman is due. It's written all over her face."

"You actually believe that book can have that much of an effect on her?"

"It's not what that book can do for her. It's the realization of what she's got that's going to smack her upside the head and transform her." The wise bookstore owner looked down at her watch. "I'd give her a good thirty minutes for the transformation to begin."

The cashier went back to getting ready for a book fair, but at the same time, questioning the owner's words. *I'll make a pass through the Green on my lunch break and see if anything's happening.*

CHAPTER 2

Jenn sat on one of the Green's benches that provided a casual spot for one to pause, reflect a moment and take a breath of the clean, fresh New England air. How invigorating it was to feel a bit closer to the serenity brought about by realizing, in the midst of the shuffle of the day, that each person was a part of the whole of creation.

On this particular late morning, the day after what had been proclaimed by all the news anchors and weather reporters as "the peak of the leaf season," she was the only person seated on the Green. The temperature was unseasonably warm, so much so that it was long-sleeve knit shirt weather.

The breeze, that customarily robbed the leaves from the trees and danced with them all the way to the ground, instead danced through Jenn's soft, wavy curls, causing her hair to look fuller than usual. Combined with the warmth of the sun, whose brightness caused a glimmering highlight in her medium-brown tresses and an iridescent sparkle in her deep-brown eyes, it seemed more like a spring day than a fall day.

She stared at the buildings that circled the Green, some of which had been there for centuries, and saw a beauty that she had never before noticed. *Isn't it strange...or rather, peacefully assuring, that less than two hours away is the hustle and bustle of the busiest city in America, and here one can be a recluse from the demands of life?*

Her insight made it easily understandable why so many of the big screen's or television's best-known celebrities found a world of seclusion in New Milford, or one of Connecticut's other nearby hideaways. She had seen several of the noted residents at community events, such as the famous Bridgewater Fair, known to the locals as the B-water Fair. They and their families would meander throughout the stands of candied apples and crafts, and watch the lumberjack and sheep-shearing exhibits just like any other family who found solitude in the rural countryside.

I wonder if they ever sit on the Green and read a

favorite book?

Jenn closed her eyes, as if the incantation of some spell were about to overtake her, and allowed her mind to clear of all inner and outer thoughts in preparation for the transformation that was soon to begin. Then she opened her eyes and methodically read the title and every word that followed, so as not to miss a single smidgen of what lay ahead. She turned page after page until, like Twain's character who left his factory job for King Arthur's legendary serfdom, she was no longer on a wooden and cast-iron bench.

It seemed the winds reached underneath her body and lifted Jenn into the air, whisking her into a slow, peaceful world of nothing but dreams as she lay back, comfortably floating, seeing and hearing the images that languidly materialized in front of her. Images of her life appeared soothingly painted on a mural for her to behold, with swift and powerful brush strokes denoting the events that had left her hurt or pained, and soft swipes for those provokingly memorable moments.

But the image that seemed to stop the moving slideshow of past photographs, and remain focused on one frame, was marked "March 5." There was only one small problem with the stopped frame. Jenn was unable to decipher whether it was 1906, 2006, or somewhere in between.

Music began to play softly in the background of her mental windmill. It was music that Jenn had heard before, and as the lyrics "Blott en dag" began, she recognized that they were Swedish, though she was unable to translate their meaning. *Ah, it's Pop singing his favorite song.* But as she sat for another moment, and listened intently to the music, the dreamer startlingly realized that she was not in 1906, 2006, or anywhere in between, and the voice she heard – at least the one singing – was not that of Pop's.

The time was 1904 in the little Swedish village of Arvika, about ten miles from the Norwegian border. It was the evening of March 5, 1904 and Jenn could hear a baby's gentle cry and see the cuddling of a mother lying on a covered mattress of straw. The father was playing the guitar and singing softly, as though to lullaby his newborn son to sleep.

Oh, my gosh! It's Pop's birthday…the day he was born. Those are his parents, Great-Grandpa Olenieus and Great-Grandmother Ida. My Gammel Farfar and Gammel Farmor.

Jenn sat totally spellbound, seeing the vision from over a century before, with snow laying on the ground outside while inside, family members huddled together in a semi-circle around the bed to see the latest addition to their family. Their excited comments were obviously compliments and blessed wishes for the infant. Women nodded and shook their heads in wonderment as the men held out their hands in comparison to the baby's and were perceptibly already sizing up the kind of manly physique the child would one day possess.

Or maybe they are trying to determine whether or not this child will have what it takes to carry on the family tradition of building and farming. To see if his hands are large enough to swing a hammer.

One by one, their attention turned from the mother and child to the father's beautiful melody and equally soothing tenor voice.

No wonder Pop was such an incredible singer. I've heard him tell tales of his parents singing and his father playing the guitar. She smiled at the vision of Pop as a newborn infant. *And he was most definitely born with good lungs,* she noted as the baby erupted into a full wail, as if trying to join his father in song.

As Olenieus fingered the simple broken chords, family members began to join him in the song, a traditional hymn they sang in their Swedish Methodist congregation. Jenn closed her eyes and let the sound fill her very being, like angelic voices of a great choir filtering through the rafters of a grand cathedral.

"Blott en dag ett ogonblick I sander, Vilken trost, evad som kommer pa!

Allt ju vilar I min Faders hander, Skulle jag, som barn, val angslas da?

Han som bar for mig en Faders hjarta, Giver ju at varje nyfodd dag

Dess beskarda del av frojd och smarta, Moda, vila och behag.

Sjalv han ar mig alla dagar nara, For var sarskild tid med sarskild nad.

Varje dags bekymmer vill han bara Han som heter bade Kraft och Rad.

Morgondagens omsorg far jag spara, Om an oviss syns min vandrings stig.

Som din dag, sa skall din kraft och vara, Detta lofte gav han mig.

Hjalp mig da att vila tryggt och stilla Blott vid dina loften, Herre kar,

Och ej trones dyra trost forspilla, Som I ordet mig forwarad ar.

Hjalp mig, Herre, att vad helst mig hander, Taga av din trogna fadershand

Blott en dag, ett ogonblick I sander, Tills jag natt det goda land."

Jenn kept her eyes closed tightly for a while after the song's ending, allowing the reverberating sounds to fade away into the distance. *Oh, that I knew what those words meant.* She longed to hear the song, or hymn as it was, once again so that she could try to interpret any of the words. As it was, she was certain that she had picked out the words for "Father" and "Mother" and "God."

What was that last phrase again? Eyes still closed, she willed her memory to replay that last phrase. *I'm sure that I can make out some sort of half-right translation for those words. I'm sure I caught the word "land" at the end.*

Land...god...goda... goda land...

That's it! "Goda land." Does that mean God's land? No... no... that can't be right. I'm sure I heard "Herre" for God. Come on, Jenn, remember those other words.

Tills...

"Tills" what?

As if a voice from heaven had heard her plea, Jenn heard the last phrase again in her head, this time as clearly as the notes on the guitar.

"Tills jag natt det goda land."

"That's it! It has to be something about a golden land. "Tills"... tills... Maybe it means something like "till I reach the golden land."

17

"It has to be a hymn about the Promised Land. A plea to the Father for the kind of guidance that will lead one to the Promised Land. That has to be right. I'm sure of it."

"Did you say something?" asked a woman, walking along the diagonal sidewalk that crossed the Green, as she turned toward Jenn's voice.

"No, I'm sorry," Jenn answered, embarrassed that she'd been heard. "I was so enthralled in trying to find a deeper understanding of this book that I guess I was thinking aloud."

The woman chuckled. "I do that quite often myself. I love to read mysteries and sometimes I get so caught up in them that I blurt the outcome aloud when I think I've solved it."

Jenn thought back on what she'd envisioned and her struggle to decipher the words. "Yes, that's almost exactly what happened to me."

The woman nodded. "Have a nice day. Enjoy the book," she called as she turned to walk away.

Suddenly, Jenn could hardly wait to pick up Samantha and ask her grandfather about the hymn. *There has to be an English translation somewhere in his house.*

She glanced over her shoulder at the front door of the library. *Or I could go in there and try to find the words online.* Jenn only took a second to change her mind about that solution.

Nope! This is a grandfather and granddaughter project. A broad smile came to her face. *Or a "Farfar - Son Dotter" project, as Grandpa would say.* Then she thought of the project from her perspective. *"A Farfar – Barns Barn" project!* Jenn loved trying to figure out the terminology for the various kinships in Swedish. *I'll take care of finding the translation the next time I visit him.*

CHAPTER 3

For some reason, Samantha's nightly bath seemed less of a chore that evening. Even the reading of her bedtime story was more enjoyable than usual. Jenn spent a few extra minutes watching her little girl drift into a restful sleep before settling down for a quiet evening.

I'm still not quite sure what it was about that book, she pondered, heading for her covered rocker where she'd laid Twain's classic, *but I don't remember a thing about what I read today.* Before she had time to turn to the last page she'd read, the phone's ringing diverted her attention. Jenn looked at the clock on the mantle. *A little early for Lindley to be calling.*

"Hello?"

"Jenn? Hi! It's Beth calling from Candlewood Valley Country Club. Glad I caught you. We've got a problem down at the restaurant. All the water from the flooding has left the golf course like a swamp. It's going to be a while before we can reopen. There are still five holes under water. We're going to have to give you the week off. With pay, of course," her boss swiftly threw in. "Enjoy some time with Samantha. I'll give you another call in a few days and let you know the status of things around here."

She laid the phone back on its base and stared at it. *An entire week of free time?* Jenn had no recollection of her last week of free time.

Seems like it must have been in a different lifetime, she jokingly mused. *At least before marriage and childbirth. Oh well, I'll have plenty of time to finish the book.*

Just as she sat in the rocker and began to read, another call interrupted her.

"How's the best mom in the world?" came the question before she had time to answer.

"Lindley!"

"I can hear in your voice that you had a successful day off. You must have gotten in that rest and relaxation you desperately needed."

"Lindley, you just won't believe,"

"I hate to cut you short, but we're having to run over tonight with the shoot. Did you kiss my little girl goodnight for me?"

"I sure did," she quickly blurted. "The flood has given me a few extra days off. I've got the whole week."

"The whole week?"

"With pay!"

"Wow! I don't have time for the details, but you ought to be the most rested and relaxed person in New Milford by the time I get back."

"More like in Connecticut," she laughed. "Call me tomorrow."

Jenn hung up the phone, amazed herself at the spunk in her voice. She started back to the chair, but the light streaming in from outside the window drew her to the front door. The moon was obviously shining brightly, but she couldn't see it from inside the house.

A few steps into the yard revealed a gorgeous full moon, basking in all its glory to announce a typical fall evening in New England. There, parading its illumination like a proud peacock showing off its plumage, was the most brilliant, yet mystical, moon Jenn had ever seen. *I should trade "A Connecticut Yankee in King Arthur's Court" for Washington Irving's "The Legend of Sleepy Hollow."*

She paced the path of the sidewalk back and forth several times as she peered into the sky. There were still traces of clouds, so many in fact, that the few holes that peeked through caused the sky to resemble a piece of delicate lace. The moon was shrouded by a film of white willowy clouds with a band of gold reflecting its light and framing it in the night sky.

My great day is pouring over into a great night. Jenn returned to the house only long enough to sneak a peek at Samantha and grab a sweater.

Her native background of growing up in the cool autumns proved to be a plus as she walked back outside to gaze at the sight of the moon. The chill of the evening failed to faze Jenn as she circled the house several times, slowly and reflectively, taking in every glimmer of the huge orb in the sky that boldly overpowered the few twinkles of stars that shone between the lacy masses of clouds.

The steps of her front porch provided the perfect landing for her to sit and watch the clouds wisp past the moon, each white patch trying to dim the glow from behind the shroud, but each unsuccessful. Its placement in the order of the firmaments clearly showed.

Jenn's thoughts moved to her grandfather. "Farfar" they had called him, ever since the family's trip to Sweden together on his 95th birthday, when they learned what Pop's family and friends called him in their native tongue.

"Their father's father," explained one of his sisters who then turned to Jenn's father, Dave, and called him, "Morfar." The sister turned back to Jenn. "That's what your children will call your father because he is their mother's father. Your children will then call Pop 'Gammel Farfar' because he is their great-grandfather. 'Gammel' means great."

Since that time, Jenn and her siblings had continued to call Pop "Grandpa," but the moment the great-grandchildren came along, he instantly became "Gammel Farfar." It had begun with Samantha's older cousin, Travis, then with her. The look on the old man's face when they called him that brought fond recollections of his native homeland, for you could see that he was also thinking of his own children's "Farfar."

She stared back up at the moon. It stood as the head, the ruler, of all the night sky. Just as her grandfather, *my "Farfar,"* stood as the head, *the patriarch,* of the Kullgren clan – a distinction that fell naturally into place in 1969 when he first returned to Sweden from America. Aware of what was forthcoming for the evening, she went inside and again checked on Samantha, making sure that her daughter was asleep and still comfortably tucked in her soft pink blanket.

Once she was content that her motherly duties were unnecessary for the next little while, Jenn went back to the front landing to allow her thoughts of the Kullgren clan to continue. *Uninterrupted*, she thought as she sat on the top step with its full vantage point of the moon. She found it extraordinarily divine that this entire day *and* evening had been like a gift from heaven.

CHAPTER 4

Tuesday

"Morfar. Go see Gammel Farfar and Morfar."

Jenn loved the joyful enthusiasm written on Samantha's face. Her daughter had reached the age where her own traits and features were taking a distinctive turn, and where inherited traits and features were noticeably visible. She'd gotten her mother's medium brown hair, combined with her father's straight locks. Her eyes were like those of her mother, her mouth like her father's, and her nose was definitely from the Kullgren side of the family.

"Later, Sammy. We'll go see Morfar and Gammel Farfar today after I pick you up," the mother promised as she fastened her daughter in the child's safety restraint of the car seat.

"Book! Go read with Gammel Farfar. Eat with Gammel Farfar." Samantha's excited little voice made it difficult for Jenn not to pass the Education Center and continue to the right turn for her parents' house, where Pop had also lived since the passing of his beloved Martha, ten years earlier.

The request was, in reality, a blessing for Jenn, for she'd been planning how to coax her little one into spending some time with Gammel Farfar that evening. The need for a hymn translation was still bouncing around in her head from the day before.

Isn't that just dandy? All that time I spent trying to invent a solution when there was no problem? I could have used my energy figuring out a clever way to get ourselves an invitation to dinner there this evening.

"How was last night's end to your free day?" Miss Erin asked when she saw Jenn and Samantha enter the Education Center.

"Better than I could have ever imagined. And you won't believe this." Jenn quickly told the teacher about the phone calls from the evening before.

"So now you can have an entire week of free days?" asked Miss Amy, hearing the news.

"That's how it appears. I really wanted to be selfish and keep Samantha all to myself, and I may do that later this week. She enjoys her playmates so much that I hate to rob her of that privilege."

"You know, Jenn," Miss Amy offered, "a little separation is good. Children have to find their own identities. Besides, the relationships they build, even at these young tender years, are good for them and their future social skills."

"I suppose you're right, but I don't want to feel like a negligent parent by leaving her here when we could be spending time together."

"You can always spend some extra time with her, but be sure to allow time for your own rest and rejuvenation. You can be a much better parent that way. And besides, you're right, Samantha loves her little friends here."

Jenn looked up to see that her daughter's coat had already been hung on its personalized peg and that the child's attention had already turned to running and playing with the other children in the room. The sight made it easy for her to anticipate another blissful morning at the park with her book.

And memories, she hoped.

"I'm sorry, Jenn. We already have plans for this evening."

Jenn felt her face drop with disappointment. She'd called her parents' house the minute she reached the Green, hoping to catch them before they made plans for dinner.

"We're fixing spaghetti for you and Samantha," her father continued. "Jean thought it would be a nice enjoyable evening for all of us if the two of you came over. Since Lindley will be gone for another day or two, this can hopefully give you a little extra time for yourself."

"I should have figured as much," mouthed Jenn softly, thinking how, so far this week, everything seemed to be out of her control.

"Excuse me?"

"Nothing… nothing, Dad. I was simply wondering whether I could bring anything?"

"Not a thing besides you and Samantha. We have it all under control."

Glad to hear it. At least I know someone's got things under control, Jenn shrugged. "Then I guess we'll see you shortly before six."

Jenn closed the cell phone and looked up in time to notice a grandfather and grandson, hand-in-hand, walking up the front steps of the New Milford Public Library to the children's section.

There's something special about grandfathers and stories, she longingly smiled as she tried to decipher which of the two had the greatest look of admiration written on his face.

She opened her book, but as had been the case the day before, the words before her eyes were from another story. Before she knew it, she was on a plane from Bradley International Airport, headed toward Newark, where she would then catch a plane to Stockholm's Arlanda Airport.

Again, like Twain's character, Jenn had been transformed to another time and place. This time, it was 1999 and she was with eight other members of her family, all on their way to Sweden to celebrate Pop's 95th birthday with his sisters and brother, and their families. She was seated beside her grandfather, and was hoping to catch a quick nap on the short flight.

He, on the other hand, was wide awake, not at all bothered by the inconvenient times of the overseas flight. *But then, this trip is a breeze compared to his first transcontinental trip, an ocean voyage that lasted for nine days in a small cabin - shared between four men - of a ship that landed him in America on his twenty-fifth birthday.* In his large palm was a small album of photographs.

Jenn watched as he studied each one long and

hard. When he saw she was awake, he smiled and held the album toward her so they could both see.

Pop turned back to the very first page. "This is the house where I lived in Arvika. Fader built the house. My uncle Knut took this picture. He and his wife, Hulda, had returned to Sweden to visit the family. See this young woman in the doorway? She is my mother, your great-grandmother, Ida Marie. The three children sitting on the railing are my two oldest sisters, Bertha and Karin, and this one is me. This is Aunt Hulda standing off to the side by herself."

The love for his family and his homeland showed in Pop's eyes and on his face as he stared at the photograph that was over ninety years old. He turned to the next page.

"This is my family when I was a child."

Jenn glared hard at the page, looking at the details of their faces. "Your parents, Pop. She is so beautiful and he is so handsome. They are a lovely couple."

"Yes." His response was quiet and simple. His gaze sharpened on the picture and Jenn could tell he was waiting to offer a more profound comment. "My mother left us when I was fourteen."

Jenn recognized that statement as a sensitive way of saying, "She died." *The very same reason we're on this flight. Grandmother "left" him.*

The granddaughter remembered how afraid the family had been of how Pop would deal with the death of his wife of sixty-three years. Jenn was in the room, only days after the memorial service, when Dave asked, "Pop, what would you like for your 95th birthday?"

The question, intended as a diversion to take the elderly man's mind off the loss of his loved one, wound up being a diversion, instead, for all of the family members trying to lessen his grief. Pop didn't blink; he didn't grieve. He didn't even stop to think.

"I want to go back to Sweden," he announced.

"Let's go!" his twin sons agreed.

Dave called one of the cousins in Sweden to tell him of Pop's request.

"Come," the cousin answered.

"I think you'd better sit down," Dave warned. "There are nine of us coming."

Jenn remembered Pop's only comment after the phone call, overheard by the entire family. "Martha would not fly. That is why we had to take the ship over in '69."

That one question, and one phone call, was how Jenn wound up, still half asleep, in the seat beside her grandfather on the plane. He had taken care of his own grieving process.

"We made it through," Pop continued. "Fader

remarried a woman that was only four years older than me."

A shudder ran through Jenn. *Did I hear this story before and forget it? I certainly don't think so. I can't imagine forgetting a tidbit of family history like that.*

"I worked with my father, Olenieus, who was a builder and a farmer. He taught me many great things, mostly how to use my hands and to enjoy and appreciate music." Pop sighed. "He and my mother were both wonderful musicians. They both sang and my father played the guitar."

Jenn realized that not only were the stories intriguing, but Pop's voice still carried the hard, thick accent of his native language after all these years. She looked at the picture of his parents, then at him, as he related his past to her. It had not dawned on her until this moment how extremely strong this man still was and how capable he was of doing whatever he desired.

She took a quick glance around the plane at some of the other elderly passengers and saw that her grandfather had no slouch; there was no weakness in his voice or in his step. *This man is quite unique.* Jenn found it hard to listen to his tale for seeing him in a new and different light.

"I can remember hearing them sing together,

my father a tenor and my mother's voice like a bird."
He rocked gently back and forth in rhythm. "My
whole family was musical. Everyone could play an
instrument and sing." He began to hum, so softly that
it was barely audible, but the melody beautiful in its
simplicity. "Ah…," Pop sighed again. "'Blott en dag.'
The first song I ever remember hearing. My parents
taught it to me when I was very young. My father
would play the guitar as he and mother sang it to
me. He was a very good musician, and used to play
and entertain at many parties."

The next page showed another view of the
house. "We cut the timber we used to build houses.
We cut the firewood for the house. It was only a small
farm. We had five or six cows and two horses."

A look of melancholy showed as he closed the
photo album and held it in his big hands. "I had a
tough time finding a job in Sweden. Finally, I accepted
there was no future for me there. Without telling my
father, I went to the travel bureau and got all my
travel passes that I would need for a passage to
America. I was twenty-three years old at the time."

"Twenty-three? I thought you were twenty-
five when you came to America."

"I was. I had the travel passes for that long
before I decided the time had come to leave. I had a
girlfriend, and the plan was that I would travel to

America, get a job, work hard and save my money, and in five years I would return to Sweden to marry her."

"But you never went back." Jenn had heard the story of how it was forty years before he returned to his homeland. "What happened?"

Pop turned and gave her that gentle smile, a common trait of his. "I had planned from the time I was twenty-three to come to America. The work at home was so sparse that I knew there was not enough for me to support a family. I got my travel passes and held onto them until I could put enough aside to make the trip. I loved my father and found it difficult to tell him that I was leaving him and the family I loved so much.

"I had heard other builders say that it was much easier to find a job in America with a Union Card, and that it was much easier to get a job if you had a card before you arrived in America. I saved my money and got one a couple of months before I left."

"The day came and I left for America. It was the middle of winter, with much snow on the ground, in February. Nine days it took back then. We landed first in Halifax, Canada. Then we came on to New York City." Pop gave a slight chuckle. "I only had two small suitcases. When my uncle picked me up, he asked, 'That's all you have?'

"I answered, 'That's all I have.'" The chuckle turned into a soft laugh. "That was all I came with to America. The clothes on my back and two small suitcases." Pop looked at Jenn with a somber stare. "I never told my father I was leaving until two months before I actually left. I never said 'good-bye.'"

Jenn waited for a moment to make sure she wasn't interrupting her grandfather's train of thought. "Okay, Grandpa, I'm confused. If you didn't tell your father that you were leaving until then, and you didn't tell him good-bye, how did your uncle know you were coming to America?"

"My father wrote to my uncle in New York, Uncle Knut, that I would be sailing for America in February. He came to the train station in Arvika to say good-bye on the day I left." Pop's voice dropped until it was barely audible. "That was the last time I saw my father. That day at the train station."

Jenn looked down at the photo album. There was her grandfather's passport from all those years ago. In the picture, Pop had a determined look in his eye, strengthened by the crossing of his arms as if to say, "I'm a man. I will make it on my own!" He was an extremely handsome man, his features prominent and his gentle compassion showing, even in his set eyes of the picture. She couldn't help but wonder whether the set eyes and jaw were merely a cover-up for his insecurity of leaving the home and family he loved.

As desperately as she wanted to know the answer, she didn't dare ask. She couldn't bear to see more sorrow than was written on his face regarding the last day with his father. The tone of his voice indicated that he dearly loved his father.

Jenn decided, instead, to change the subject. "Uncle Knut. He's the one that took the picture of your house in Arvika, right?"

"That's right!" Pop launched into that enthusiastic voice he was known to use when one of his grandchildren had finally caught on to something. "Uncle Knut found out when I would arrive and met me at the harbor. A minister from one of the local churches came to meet everyone who came without anyone to meet them. There were many like that, but my aunt and uncle were there for me."

"But what about the girlfriend?"

"You should know the answer to that, my child. I met your grandmother, Martha, after I came here."

Their conversation was interrupted by the announcement of the plane's approach of the airport. *I'll have to hear the rest of this story later*, Jenn told herself.

The curious granddaughter was anxious to hear about how her grandparents, married sixty-three years before her grandmother's death, met. Jenn knew there was nothing she was hearing for the first time. Pop had always been glad to talk about his younger days, his family and his homeland. But this was the first time that she had actually put all the pieces together. This trip made a great backdrop for the "puzzle," as she saw it. *Besides, I need to know all this before we get there. I'll have a much clearer understanding of things when we arrive and I meet everyone.*

Jenn was ready to go back to the girlfriend and her grandmother, but Pop wanted to talk about his arrival to the "New World."

"I'd not had a haircut since I left Sweden, so Uncle Knut took me to a barber shop and translated for me that I wanted a haircut. I didn't have any decent clothes to get a job, so then he took me to a men's clothier and bought me a whole new suit and a hat and an overcoat. That was quite a welcome to a new country!"

There was a pause. It was clear that Pop was reliving the experience in his mind. "Yep. It was a good time. He helped me get my first job in a large factory where he worked. He asked the foreman if there was anything I could do. When I got out that day, Uncle Knut asked me what the foreman said."

Pop gave a big laugh. "Ta kosten feje. Take the broom and sweep." He laughed again. "'Take the broom and sweep' was the first job I had. To keep the floor clean. The foreman was Norwegian, so I could understand what he said."

"He spoke Swedish?"

"No, I understood Norwegian. Arvika was very close to the border. In May, Uncle Knut went back to Sweden. He gave me his mandolin before he left. Do you remember seeing it at home on the top of my dresser?"

"That wooden instrument with the rounded back? Of course, I remember it. It's beautiful." She didn't bother to tell him that when they returned to New Milford, it would be sitting on the dresser, re-strung and waiting for him as a birthday present.

"Yes, it is. I told you my whole family was musical. Uncle Knut bought it when he came to America. He was afraid it would get broken on the ship, so he left it with me. I never learned to play it, but I loved it just the same. It reminded me of my family and all the music I'd heard all my life grow-ing up in Sweden."

Pop smiled and nodded. "When Uncle Knut left, he dropped me off at his sister's, my moster. That means she was my mother's sister, my maternal aunt, my Aunt Ellen. She had an apartment in New York

City on the east side. At the corner of 67th Street and 3rd Avenue." His eyes showed that in his mind was a vision of the apartment and the corner, exactly as they had been when he was twenty-five.

"Although she had no children, Aunt Ellen had adopted a boy. I shared a bedroom with him. Bobby, that was his name. Years later, after my Aunt Ellen had raised him and given him a good life, Bobby joined the Army and got married before leaving for World War II. During the course of the war, he was missing on a flight from Africa and was never located. His wife got the money from the government and his family got nothing."

Pop sat quietly again, this time focusing his eyes on the in-flight movie. It was obvious that his eyes were looking past the screen as he thought of Bobby and his sad misfortune.

Jenn desperately wanted to get back to the subject of how he met her grandmother, but did not want to distract him from important parts of his memories. There would be time for her questions later.

He leaned his head back against the seat, then reclined it and pulled the blanket over his lap.

Ninety-five years of memories. I may never get him back on the subject of meeting my grandmother.

Jenn reopened the album that Pop had handed her after the story about Bobby. She leafed through all the photos, deciphering the family connections and the events. It seemed she had barely flipped to the last page when she heard Pop's voice, again full of exuberance. *I sure hope I inherited his tenacity and quality of life*, she thought as she flashed a giant smile.

Before she had time to broach the subject of "the girl who was left behind," Pop pulled the album from her hands and turned to a couple of pages past where he'd left off. His tale, however, continued as if he'd never stopped.

"I later got a job mixing cement. When I asked the foreman at that job what I was supposed to do, he only spoke English. I knew no English, so I had to watch the other workers and try to figure out what he had told me. One of the other workers came over and explained to me what to do. I did okay. Every day I'd see what the other men were doing, and when the foreman gave me my orders, I did exactly what the others did."

Pop's face broke into a huge grin, proud of the game he'd played.

And won! Jenn thought proudly.

"I had a good time for I had a job. It was a forty-hour week. I had to work some every day, and half a day on Saturday and Sunday, too. It was at a place way downtown past Wall Street, near Battery Park.

"There were some bad times, too, though. You

had to wear your good clothes to work, then put on overalls. Then you'd get dressed again in your good clothes when you were finished. One Saturday, it came time to go home. I went to get dressed and my clothes were gone. All the money I had was in them. So was the big watch and chain that my father had given me before I left for America. All gone."

Jenn sat speechless. *How could anyone take the only thing from home that this dear man owned?*

"It was a hard time back then. I had a different job another time on 58th Street, putting up paneling in a house. I only had two pairs of shoes. One to wear to work and another pair to work in. While I was working, someone took my good shoes and left me with their old ones. They were full of holes on the bottom, and I had to walk home in them. At that time, I lived up in East Harlem on 128th Street."

Pop noticed the look of horror on Jenn's face. "The neighborhood was much different then."

Jenn nodded in understanding.

"It was raining very hard and my feet were completely soaked by the time I got home. Not a dry stitch on me." He nodded back at Jenn. "Yep. It was a hard time. But I made it through." Pop barely paused before he began another story.

"There was another day that I was eating in a small restaurant. In those days, you would have a raincoat in the spring and a heavier overcoat in the winter. I had a nice Swedish overcoat, one I'd brought from home, and a straw hat, which I hung on the coat rack. Some person took my coat and hat, and left an old overcoat in its place. They took it right behind my back. Right behind me!"

The elderly man shook his head with a quiet sigh. "I didn't wear the old shabby coat. I left it hanging right on the coat rack."

Jenn laughed heartily at her grandfather's spunk. Since she'd been old enough to know him, Pop had always possessed a great sense of pride in whom and what he was. *I see some things haven't changed.*

"There was a good thing that happened because I joined the Union before I left Sweden, even though the dues for the card cost me about one or two month's wages at the time. When I arrived in New York City, I was going to join the local Scottish Carpenter's Union on the West Side. I took the book and to get in the local Carpenter's Union, it only cost me ten dollars since I already had my card. It was usually two or three hundred dollars to join in the city.

"There was a bank on 42nd Street, across from Grand Central Station. My aunt took me down there and I put in money." Pop grinned, proud that he had managed his funds well. "That was the first time I had ever been inside a bank. She taught me to go down there every week when I got paid and put in some of the money.

"Third Avenue also had a Swedish grocery store. They sold everything there." His voice gave way to a lighthearted energy as he settled into this conversation just as he had settled into living in America.

Pop looked down at the picture on the page that lay open in front of him. It was a photograph of him as a young man. He had his arm around a young woman and there was another couple in the picture.

"This is me and Martha right after we were married."

The granddaughter stared down at the picture. "This is grandmother?"

"Yes. My Martha."

Jenn loved the way her grandfather said the word "Martha." There was a Swedish pronunciation of the "th" sound that made it come out sounding almost like "Marta." There was such a beautiful ring to it, and the way Pop said it, there was also a rhythmical lilt to it, not to mention the caress that was still evident in his voice when he spoke of her.

The granddaughter stared down at the picture. Pop's charm and dashingly good looks were captured by the camera. It seemed funny to her to see this couple, very much in love, whom she had known only as grandparents. She had caught the gleam in their eyes when they would look at each other, but certainly nothing of the nature that she saw in the photograph.

And Grandpa… look how tall and handsome. So distinguished. I'm surprised his girlfriend in Sweden ever let him get away. She reached her finger out and touched the picture of her grandmother. *How different life seems now without her.*

Looking intently at the photograph, Jenn saw where she got her brown waves and the shape of her face. However, the question still haunted her.

How did you meet my grandmother? she wanted to scream, which she probably would have done had they not been closed up on an airplane with over a hundred other people.

"There were three Swedish churches in New York City when I arrived. One Methodist, one Mission and one Baptist. I attended the Swedish Methodist church because that is what I had attended at home."

Jenn could tell from the tender reflectiveness in Pop's voice that this was one of the sweetest memories of his life. *And I'll bet it has something to do with how he met "his Martha."*

"Ladies and gentlemen," announced the

plane's captain. "We have been cleared for landing and will be at the gate in approximately ten minutes."

The rest of the words were missed as Jenn watched everyone on the plane making a mad dash to the lavatories, picking up belongings and peering anxiously at the ground below them. Pop closed his photo album and asked her to place it in his small carry-on bag.

Looks like that's all of the story I'm going to get for one flight, she concluded as Pop watched the antics of the passengers around him as if they were part of a three-ring circus.

And that was all of a daydream Jenn was going to get for one morning on the Green, for her stomach beckoned that it was time for lunch.

A Clams Casino pizza at the Holiday sounds good. With that thought, she left the wooden park bench and her transatlantic memory.

CHAPTER 5

"I wanted to sit next to Grandpa," Jenn whined.

"You already sat next to Grandpa. It's my turn," Tom informed her.

"Hey, Tom, what seat are you in?" called David.

"We're on the row with Grandpa. The three seats by the window. Let's have him in the middle so he can tell us all about Sweden."

"Why don't you two guys let Pop sit next to the aisle," suggested Dave as he made his way down the jet's aisle behind them.

"But, Dad," Jenn wanted to say. She saw it was no use.

"How did you manage to get us seats that are separated?" a woman scolded her husband. She sat down across the aisle from Pop, huffing and puffing as if there were some great inconvenience.

The husband moved closer to Jenn until he stopped and began comparing the seat number on his ticket with the numbers above the seats. "Excuse me," he apologized, stepping over her. "I'm in the seat next to you."

Dave, having heard the commotion and watching the wife follow her husband with her eyes, leaned over the seat.

"Sir, if you'd like to sit by your wife, I'm sure my daughter wouldn't mind switching seats with her. My father and sons are across the aisle from your wife."

"Are you sure you don't mind?" the man asked in Jenn's direction.

She didn't even bother to answer, but took off toward his wife's seat, lest he change his mind and welcome the silence.

Jenn had returned to the Green from lunch to find her bench from the morning vacant. She no more than sat down when her mind picked up from where the memories had left off less than two hours earlier. The granddaughter was again whisked away and recreating a scene on an airplane, but this time she was on a much longer flight from Newark to Stockholm, still in quest of how her grandparents met.

"I thought we'd gotten rid of you," Tom playfully threw past Pop when his youngest sibling switched seats with the woman across the aisle.

A "leave-me-alone" glare was all he got in return. Jenn was too busy hoping she could get back into the conversation with Pop about his early days in America.

"I'll bet *you* never got to caddy for Grandpa," teased Tom, directing his words to David. He was the grandchild with the sense of humor and a comment for everything. His teases were playful rather than tormenting. Pop wouldn't have allowed it any other way.

"No, but I got to play plenty of games of minigolf with him at that little course behind the Ski Haus," bragged David. "We always got a soda after the game."

"That was nothing." Before David had a chance to respond to his older brother's taunt, Tom, in the middle of the three seats, turned toward Pop. "Remember all those summer days you let me caddy for you at the golf course? The minute we'd get out of sight from the clubhouse, you'd let me play."

"Now that was some fun," Tom directed to

David, rubbing it in more. He turned back to Pop. "I may have been exposed to a little too much foul language from some of the other golfers, but those were some of the best days a boy could have!"

Pop smiled. "Yep. Those were the days."

"According to you, Pop, all the days you talk about were 'the days.'"

"Yep. That's how I've always lived my life. One day at a time."

Tom looked back to David. "Remember how Pop could always bring us to his knees by using his thumb and index finger on our wrists?"

"He didn't ever have to do that to me." David could hardly hold back the laughter as he took this opportunity to joke with his brother.

"Oh, yes, he did," chimed in Jenn. "I saw him."

"The only reason he didn't do it to you was because you were the baby. Nobody ever did anything to you," Tom retorted in a sing-song fashion.

"Oh, yes, they did," she defended. "Grandma let me do stuff with her all the time. Like making cinnamon buns."

"Boy, I can taste Grandma's cinnamon buns now," Dave smiled. "She could bake anything."

"All I remember about the kitchen," laughed Tom, "was how we'd sit on the tall stool in the kitchen to help Grandma, and Grandpa would always say,

'One never sits while baking.'"

"I think we all heard that," Dave nodded.

"One never sat and did much of anything with Grandpa. It was like he was still the foreman at work, and we were the crews working under him at the United Nations Building."

"Eight hours of work for eight hours of wages," Pop said. It was a phrase all three grandchildren had heard repeatedly during their lives. "I was always taught to give an honest day's work."

"The first time I ever heard you say that, Grandpa," Tom said, "was when we were working on some construction project at the house. I always had to be the 'gofer' and I must have complained about something. I don't remember if it was when we converted the garage into the living room, built the new garage, or built the fence around the pool."

This time David knew he had Tom licked. "The first time I heard that phrase was when we put new shingles on the roof. How I hated carrying those shingles up the ladder to the roof. I must have said something about it, because Grandpa's only words were, 'eight hours of work for eight hours of wages.' I wanted to remind him I wasn't getting a penny, but I knew if I did, I'd hear how much work he had already done by my age."

Jenn listened to her brothers bat comments

back and forth with their grandfather until the plane's interior lights were turned off. She learned all kinds of things that she'd missed along the way, being the youngest and a girl, but she still missed out on finding out how Harry and Martha met.

Surely someone in Sweden will know that story. Then she realized that Pop waited forty years to return to his homeland. *Who there would know anything about my grandmother? I may go through my entire life never knowing how my grandparents met!*

She went to sleep hoping to wake up earlier than her brothers and have her grandfather all to herself.

"Can you believe it took me nine days to cross the ocean by ship and now they can fly me home in ten hours?"

Jenn heard the familiar voice and opened her eyes. Pop was talking to the steward while everyone else slept. *Ah, now's my chance.*

The plane's lights came on as a stewardess started down the aisle with a basket of warm washclothes.

Mumblings and groanings were heard from

some of the passengers who had missed their beauty sleep, while other passengers were totally oblivious to the movement going on around them.

"If you get up after six, you've wasted half the day," Pop said to her.

"But Pop," Jenn defended, looking at her watch, it's only 5 in the morning.

"Good! That gives us another hour to look forward to seeing our family."

Good! she tried to convince herself. *That gives me an hour to find out how they met.* Jenn's plan was once again foiled as she saw the carts of breakfasts moving up the aisle.

"Is it time to eat?" Tom sat up and looked around. "Good! I'm starved."

I'm glad everyone is getting what they want this morning, Jenn sarcastically huffed. *Too bad I didn't let the woman stay in this seat. I'd have found out just as much.*

Within an hour, the plane was on the ground. For the first time, Jenn realized that she didn't know how to say "hello" to anyone.

Not to worry! I'll simply do like Grandpa on his cement job and follow everyone else's lead.

She grabbed her backpack from the overhead compartment and followed her brothers to the start of a wondrous "homecoming."

CHAPTER 6

Jenn sat down at the table and as her family joined hands and recited the usual Swedish blessing, it was hard for her to get the afternoon's image of Tom and David from her mind. Her effort wasn't helped by the fact that there was relatively little or no change in either of her brothers.

Tom's black hair still looked the same, style and all, for he, like all the rest of the grandchildren on that trip, had been primed and shaped into his best appearance possible in preparation for meeting the rest of Pop's clan.

Jenn chuckled at this flashback, for while they were waiting in Newark for their connecting flight, one of the adults reminded all the grandchildren that, "When you get there, you want to put your best foot forward." The youngest of her cousins had looked down at her feet and immediately asked, "How do you know which is the best one?"

Looking back on that adventure, it had brought even her stateside family closer together through a bond they'd have never achieved otherwise. Sure, they could have gone to a farm or on a retreat, like Pop did with relatives in the years when his children were youngsters. But the same depth of kinship would not have developed.

The trip to Sweden had allowed each of the Kullgren's to get a taste of their heritage – the Americans for the Swedish backbone; the Swedish for the American influence. It had, besides being one of life's greatest pleasures for all of the Kullgren's, been a tremendous learning experience and an appreciation for all Pop had accomplished in his lifetime.

One man. A single lifetime, Jenn contemplated.

Now as she sat looking across the table at that patriarch who was loved and claimed by so many, she understood the scripture that she had heard from the pulpit on the past Sunday. The scripture she had heard so much in her lifetime that it was practically memorized. She thought she knew it before, but as she watched Pop eat – still in that European style of using his left hand and the knife to arrange his food into nice-sized bites and pile it onto the right hand's fork – the passage from Matthew 5 now took on definition… real meaning… meaning through action.

"Blessed are the poor in spirit… Blessed are they that mourn… Blessed are the meek… Blessed are they which hunger and thirst after righteousness… Blessed are the merciful… Blessed are the pure in heart… Blessed are the peacemakers…,"

Jenn stared at Pop in complete admiration. What she saw was a man who was a child of God who had been filled and comforted by God's mercy throughout his life. He had walked peaceably through every joy and every tribulation of his life's journey, singing the same song of rejoicing and exceeding gladness for each of them. He had seen God at every corner of the earth he had inherited. There was no doubt that his reward truly did lay in the kingdom of heaven.

Pop is blessed. He is truly blessed. He is surrounded by loved ones in a house, a physical home. He is surrounded by loved ones around the world, relatives who dwell in countries around the globe. He is…,

"Are you okay, Jenn?" Dave asked. "You haven't touched a bite of your food."

"Oh…," Her father's question drew her back into the family feast as she quickly twirled a huge bite of spaghetti around her fork and shoved it into her mouth, trying to catch up with the others. Swallowing hard, she twirled another bite with her fork. "I guess I was thinking about making Tom and David wait for dessert."

"Impossible," chided Tom. "Since when do you think?" He winked at his younger sister.

Jenn wanted to provide him with a playful retaliation, but as she looked into her older brother's eyes, she saw an inherent feature from Pop that she'd never before noticed. Underneath that layer of relentless teasing and taunting were eyes that said he would drop everything and go to bat for her. Eyes that said he adored his young niece, Samantha, who sat beside him, leaning against his arm.

"You're nothing but a big teddy bear, you know. I can see right through your cutting words." Her reply brought about more of a "touché" than any insult she could have given, for it left Tom speechless, a trait she seldom saw in him.

Jenn took a good look at her other brother, the middle child of the family. The only real difference in David that had occurred over the years was that his crew-cut, a part of his soccer player image, had been traded for a shorter haircut for his police career. There was still that look of determination in his face, accented by his strong jaw and steel-gray eyes.

The same jaw and eyes that were in Grandpa's passport! she suddenly realized. His naturally tanned skin and muscular physique perfectly suited his personality and profession.

Outwardly, the three of them were no more alike than they had been on that airplane for Pop's 95th birthday celebration. *But inwardly,* she reflected, *we are all of the same ilk.*

Jenn got up from the table to serve one of Pop's favorite desserts, strawberry-rhubarb pie, with her thoughts on Samantha and the hope that her young daughter would one day claim her right to inherit Pop's temperament and philosophy of life.

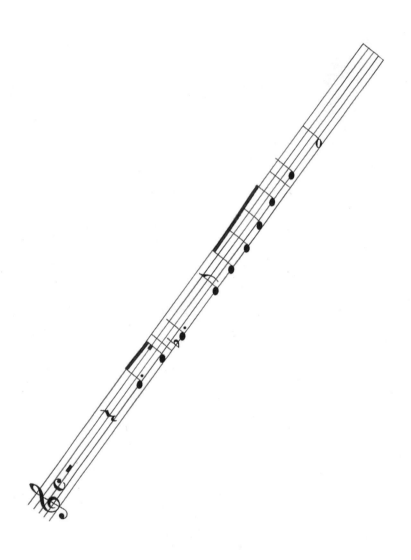

PART TWO

SUMMER

A time of vibrant zest and glorious splendor
the whole world is green and branches strong
the sun so bright there seems no tomorrow

Pride and confidence in youthful pleasures
covering one's eyes from any dangers
ready to face the world and all within it

CHAPTER 7

Wednesday

The arrival of Wednesday brought about a great event in the life of the Kullgren's. Dave and Jean had left for the Finger Lakes early that morning and, later in the week, would travel on to Vermont for their annual "leaf trek" with Jean's best friend. It was an outing they looked forward to every fall, and one that had been a tradition for nearly twenty years.

It was also an outing that their children looked forward to every fall for it meant the visit of Dave's twin brother, their Uncle George, from Maryland. The siblings always got together for a grand and glorious reunion during the week that he was in New Milford. A time of catching up had already been scheduled for this evening, at least in Jenn's mind.

This will probably be Samantha's first time to remember Uncle George when she grows up. She was only an infant the last time she saw him. That brought to mind the first time Jenn remembered meeting her Uncle George. At that point in time, he and her father, who were identical twins, still fit the bill of "identical." The past two decades had robbed them of a bit of that distinctive honor and finally awarded them each their own identities.

Jenn could hardly wait to show her daughter the photograph of the two men as toddlers. *They must have been about the same age Samantha is now.* She pictured the curls on the two boys. *Curls that I inherited,* she grinned as she looked in the mirror of the van's sun visor.

For the moment, she had to settle for another morning of "waking up" with the day's specialty of the Bank Street Coffee House. *And then a flood of more memories of life with Pop.*

She dropped Samantha off at the Education Center, shared a brief conversation with Miss Amy and Miss Erin and then headed toward the Green. *It feels more like home this week than my living room!* she chuckled, tempted to count down the days until she had to go to work, but hastily admonishing that idea for fear of losing any "quality time."

What gorgeous weather! The morning drive had Jenn in awe of the beautiful weather that seemed to only be getting better with each passing day. *I hope Mom and Dad have this same weather on the Finger Lakes.* She thought of her uncle's arrival. *And Uncle George for his drive here.* She imagined both of them driving in such magnificent areas of the country and what the views must look like with the leaves in full majesty, the sun's bright rays giving them a glorious golden radiance.

So much for spending the morning in the coffee house. I'll get it, sit on the Green and watch the cars pass.

"Watch the cars pass?" Since when have you ever just sat and watched the cars pass, Jenn Kullgren? She laughed aloud as she parked her car in one of the Green's diagonal parking spaces. *Maybe more of Pop is rubbing off on you than you realized!* Jenn walked toward Bank Street, a bit more chipper than she had been all week.

All week? Try all year! she beamed as she opened the door of the coffee shop and greeted the young man behind the counter. "How about something as special as this morning is?"

"You got it," he nodded and turned to create a beverage just for her.

Jenn sat on the bench, the one that she had marked as hers for the week, facing Route 7. The weather seemed to have brought about an aura in the air, an aura that spread much farther than any temperature or barometric pressure or such. All of the sun and its warmth, for this late in the year, brought about an emotional and mental state in the residents and passersby that was evident even in their walk or the way they drove around the Green.

Kind of like the lazy, hazy days of summer are still here. Or rather, have come back for one last visit before departing for another year, leaving the earth to change its course, to change its season.

Jenn began to reflect on her life, short in comparison to Pop's, long in comparison to Samantha's. *Like seasons, one's life is.* She saw Samantha in her mind, running and playing with her little friends on the plastic sliding board at the Education Center. *I wonder what Pop did when he was a toddler. I wonder if there was that same poised stature of his walk and his stance.* She tried to recall the scenery of Arvika, both from Pop's photo album and from her memories of the past two days.

I suspect that he ran and played along the countryside. Jenn wondered about the relationships he had with his siblings and how different it must have been for him as the older brother from what it was for her as the baby sister. *I guess that makes me similar to his sister, Nancy.*

I wonder if he ever got into disagreements with his siblings. She grinned. *After all he is a bit stubborn.* Her grin turned into a chuckle. "The stubborn Swede," she mouthed, thinking of the nickname the family sometimes called Pop. *Well, that's one trait that Samantha and I got honestly.* It was then that she thought of her first black eye, with Tom holding her and David kneeing her. *Must have been during one of our heated soccer or football games in the front yard.*

Jenn shook her head at the thought. *Naw, Grandpa is too patient to have done that. He'd have been showing his siblings how to do something.* Another smile crossed her lips. *Probably something connected with work.*

She thought of Pop's work ethic. *And I suppose that he learned to milk the cow at a very early age, and swing an ax, and hammer a nail... why, I bet he could hammer a nail as soon as he could talk! No wonder he never started a project that he didn't finish.* "Follow through," he'd always say to the grandchildren. "Don't start something you don't finish."

Spring. That was the spring of his life. When everything with which he came in contact was painted with the newness of life... or at least a newness to his life.

Jenn pictured herself in the spring of her own

life. The vision that stood out the most was a visit to Florida to visit her grandparents. They played cards – *Liverpool Rummy*, she recalled – for hours. She thought of the way they'd play nine or ten different hands of the game, that became known as their family card game, as they'd move from one level to the next with each hand.

And there was always lots of food. Grandma never lost her knack of creating a smorgasbord for us. Jenn's memory moved to how Tom, David and she would draw straws to see which one had to sit beside their grandfather. No one wanted to sit next to him, for he'd fill up their plate and they were not allowed to leave the table until they ate everything on the plate. *Now we like to fill up his plate and watch him eat all of it*, she smiled with great admiration.

Her admiration came from the many positive attributes she could list for him. His kindness. His outgoing way of treating everyone he met the same. *Even those he doesn't know.* She smiled as she thought of his generosity and how she'd seen his habit in action as he constantly thought of others.

Jenn thought back to his patience of handling the grandchildren, and now the great-grandchildren. *I wonder if he had that same patience with Dad and Uncle George?* That was another question she expected to have an answer for before the end of the week.

And then there's the subject of faith. Pop and his church. How many times she'd heard about how many services he attended each Sunday. His church was his life. *His church is still his life, even though he doesn't get to go as often as he once did. His church is sitting in his recliner and singing his beloved hymns. The same ones he's sung over and over for years in choirs wherever he lived.* Jenn longed for Samantha to inherit a bit of that faith. She vowed to make that example a top priority on her list for child rearing. *Just as Grandpa and Grandma did for their two sons.*

She laid her head back against the bench. The sun beat down on her brow, hinting at a last reminder of the summer's warmth. Jenn looked up into the sun. *Summer. How soon it fades into the distance.*

Her thoughts turned to her own life. For her, she was in summer. Life was full as she had given birth to a little one of her own. She was aware of many of the dangers and trials of life, but she was still too young to let them burden her daily cares. Energy was mixed with carefree moments, *like now*, when there was a self-aspiring ego telling her what she needed to do to reach her goals in life, backed by a momentum to still carry out those goals.

Clickety-clack, clickety-clack.

Jenn looked from the sun to the sidewalk where a teenager was riding down the concrete on his skateboard. *No worries. No cares. No thoughts of tomorrow.* She smiled as the teen rode out of sight around the corner at the far end of the Green.

Now he's *moving from spring into the summer. Still wet behind the ears – although not to hear him tell it, I'm sure! – but past the gangly days of his limbs and size not being exactly in sync. In control of his movements – and his life, if you asked him, I'll bet! – to the extent that he knows where he wants to go and has some kind of image of how he wants to get there.*

She smiled to herself. *Reality has not yet sunk in, I'm afraid.*

Jenn pictured herself at that age of going from her spring to her summer. Just as the adolescent had left the Green, she was now mentally on her way to Helena, Georgia on a hot summer's day, about fifteen years before. The sun was beating down on her face and she pulled down the hot pink hat that she had gotten that day on a shopping spree with her grandmother. It had bright pink lips on the top of the hat and had been one of her cherished treasures at that juncture of life. Wherever she went that summer, the hat was a part of her wardrobe.

Her height, which she inherited from both Pop and Martha, had graced her with long limbs, perfect for playing girls' basketball. However, they were not used to always working together yet. She envisioned the picture of her in her soccer uniform, from about that same time, with the black shorts and the forest green shiny top with the name of her team screened in large white letters.

Not a care in the world as I ran and kicked the ball with all my might. Kicking it the same as I kicked everything else that got in my way of having a good time or reaching my dream. My dream of going to college, getting married and one day having a family of my own.

Suddenly, Jenn was back on the bench with the summer-like warmth kissing her skin. In all aspects of the word, she had reached her dream. She had a college degree. She had a beautiful wedding with relatives from all over the world showing up for it. And she had a family of her own.

But do I have all there is to life? Have I attained the most important goal in life?

Clickety-clack, clickety-clack.

Jenn looked up in time to see the skateboarder coming back around the corner, a soda in his hand, as he balanced himself on the wooden board, one foot in front of the other.

One foot in front of the other. One step at a time. Exactly as Pop walked through each day of his life. Day by day.

Suddenly, the sound of the skateboard's wheels was no longer the focal point of her attention. *Day by day… "Blott en dag…,"*

That's it. Those are the words I was trying so hard to remember. Jenn recalled the day – *that same day that I was in his front yard at the house in Orange Grove, Florida – that he began to sing that song. I stopped him…* *"Grandpa, what does that song mean?"*

Jenn had no recollection of the rest of the words, but simply that first phrase that meant, "Day by day and with each passing moment."

That's the most important goal to attain in life. That's when one has reached their dream. When the simplicity of life is realized and grabbed, like a tiger by the tail, except instead of barreling through life at the pace of a charging tiger, one puts one foot in front of the other and walks humbly through life…day by day.

From out of nowhere, Jenn heard a sound – probably nothing but a gentle wind rustling through the limbs above – but it seemed to say, "Have you reached that goal, Jenn? Have you ascertained your ultimate dream in life and gone after it?" She looked up at the sky, at the sun that earlier had warmed her face and hands.

The words were from her subconscious she was sure, but she couldn't help but wonder if they had not been instigated with a little help from above.

"That's a goal one never reaches, isn't it, God?" she prayed silently. *"Not until he's walked through life*

with you hand in hand like Grandpa. Not until he's passed through the spring and the summer and the autumn. And he sits in the winter of life and looks back and realizes his greatest accomplishment was to have reached the point of taking it all one day at a time as it came to him.

Jenn stared back at the teenager, who had stopped at the bandstand, climbed its steps, taken a seat and was now staring out across the Green. To look at him, his eyes taking in all that lay in front of him, the children at play, the shoppers, the library patrons, people going to the bank, the post office, the drug store, the lawyer's office, the restaurants – even the funeral parlor – he was getting a magnificent view of every slice that life had to offer.

A much different perception of seeing the world than from speeding down the sidewalk on a skateboard, one foot firmly planted on the board, the other kicking madly trying to make the rider go faster and faster.

Kind of like life, she reasoned. *The left foot and the right foot are not moving in sync with each other. They are not going through life with one foot in front of the other. And when God has provided us with a wonderful life, we want to try to kick it away with one foot while we go where we want with the other.*

Pretty soon, the teenager was joined by his friends, all of whom had shown up to congregate at the bandstand.

They're out of school already? It wasn't until then that Jenn sensed her stomach trying to get a word in edgewise amidst her thoughts.

"Jenn?"

She also hadn't noticed that a close family friend had walked up behind her. "Roberta! I didn't hear you. I'm sorry. I guess my mind was off in space somewhere." *That's where it has been most of this week.*

"How are you? And how's Pop?"

"I'm fine, and Pop's the same as he always is. 'I'm fine, everything's fine' is that response I get every time I ask him." Jenn's face broke into a soft smile as a look of discovery came upon her. "You know, I'm a grown woman with a daughter of my own and that's the only answer I've ever heard from him when asked how he was. Then he goes on with, 'One day at a time. Yep. I just take it one day at a time.'"

Roberta Buddle had been friends with the Kullgren's for a long time. Her son, since middle school, had been best friends with Tom. They stayed in touch and still went on golfing outings together. She also attended the same church, so she knew Pop well and had most definitely heard him use that same phrase. Now it was her turn to smile.

"I'm sure that was exactly how he felt then, and still does. People can't live that long, and have as full a life as Pop has had, if they feel otherwise. A

73

large part of that quality of life is his attitude and his faith, you know."

Jenn cocked her head slightly and nodded. "Yes, I don't think I did know that before ... or ever even thought about it ... but I believe you must be right."

She thought of the difference in her attitude of this morning and the attitude she'd possessed on Monday morning. When she stopped to compare, she saw herself as a different person. Those around her saw and heard the difference on the outside – as Miss Amy, Miss Erin and Lindley commented – but she felt the difference on the inside.

"Okay, Grandma!" called a red-haired girl, who possessed the same exuberance for life and the same wavy locks that Jenn had at that young adolescent age. "I'm through at the library."

Obviously in her summer of life, too! Jenn noted. *She even has on a basketball jersey like I used to wear.*

"Tori, this is Jenn McCaughan. She's the sister of your dad's friend, Tom," explained Roberta.

Using her best manners, Tori gave a quick wave. "Hi, how are you?"

"'I'm fine, everything's fine,'" Jenn said, this time in the form of a pronouncement rather than a statement.

"Yes, you are and it is," Roberta confirmed.

"Tori and I were just on our way to The Hearth for a late lunch. Would you like to join us? I'll be glad to bring you back here on my way home."

Jenn thought for a moment. "Yes, I think I would, thank you. A good meat-and-potatoes lunch would hit the spot about right now." Her stomach agreed with the answer.

They crossed the Green to Roberta's car.

"Tori, did you know that Tom's and Jenn's grandfather is going to be 102 on his next birthday?"

"Get outta town!"

Jenn laughed at Tori's expression of surprise. *Ah, that age of using lots of unique sayings.* She tried to remember what her favorite expression had been in the early summer of her life.

This young woman is in the process of discovering the meaning of life. Roberta gazed at the cloudless sky backdrop behind the hillside in the distance. *May she always follow in the path of her grandfather*, were the words of her silent prayer.

His attitude and his faith, huh? Jenn's spirit matched the brightness of the blue sky hovered over the Green, an uncommon sight for this time of year in New Milford. *May I always exemplify Pop's attitude and faith for my own child*, Jenn prayed in silence, for the second time that day.

CHAPTER 8

*D*on't tell me that someone has taken my bench! Jenn noticed as she closed the door of Roberta's car. *What was it Tori said, "Get outta town!" That's what I should go and tell that person. I should just walk over there and tell them that they are interfering with my right of self-preservation.*

"Jenn!"

Was I thinking that loudly? The person on the bench was calling her name. She walked closer and saw that the woman on the bench was her cousin, Linnea.

"Lin! I didn't recognize you at first."

"I saw you staring at me, but there was a blank

gaze on your face."

Jenn didn't bother to explain the blank stare.

Linnea was more like an aunt than a cousin, for she was close to the same age as Dave and George, and they had literally grown up doing everything together.

"Did your parents get gone this morning?"

"Yes, and Uncle George is on his way here."

"I'll have to get by to see him this week. How's Pop doing?" Lin immediately laughed. "Never mind, don't tell me. "I'm fine, everything's fine. It's too bad everyone can't go through life with Uncle Harry's way of taking things one day at a time."

"You've known him your whole life, haven't you, Lin?"

"Sure have. He brought me home from the hospital. Our families practically lived together. I was the daughter they didn't have. We went to church every Sunday and then ate lunch at our house one week, and Uncle Harry's the next. Then after lunch, we'd take long walks together. That was the way it was my whole life growing up.

"We even took vacations together. Every summer, we'd all pack into my father's 2-door Pontiac. Uncle Harry and Aunt Martha, my parents, the two boys and me, and off we'd go to Marquette. It took three days to get there and three days to get back.

We'd spend anywhere from four to six weeks in the upper peninsula of Michigan at Froling's Farm. It was an old farmhouse and all the families there were Swedish. Boy, did we have fun."

"I've heard my dad speak of that farm. He said family members would come from everywhere to visit."

"They sure would. We'd have tons, literally tons, of company. They'd come for a day or a week, but they all came. One uncle arrived every summer in his latest Cadillac, with his rowboat in tow. We kids looked forward to that each year.

"We'd set up make-shift beds and cots all over the farmhouse. Hi-jinks and laughter prevailed the whole time, and your grandmother was usually the one who started it all. If your bed was short-sheeted, you'd need look no further. You knew Aunt Martha was involved."

Lin burst into laughter. "That's probably what saved our hides when George and Dave and I colored the bedroom ceiling, punched a child-size hole through the wall, and turned the hose on through the kitchen window."

"You three did that?" Jenn couldn't believe her ears. "I never heard that story before."

"I'm sure you didn't. We all swore we'd never mention it until you were all grown and wouldn't try those pranks yourselves." Lin was still howling with laughter.

They were in the summers of their lives. Jenn thought of a tale from her generation when the grandchildren had made a pact never to tell what happened.

"Then I guess it's safe now for David to tell Dad and Grandpa what he did one summer. We were visiting Grandma and Grandpa and they had a group of friends over. They were sitting around eating cake and drinking coffee and David and I got bored.

"David decided it would be great fun to pass the time riding Grandpa's bicycle around the neighborhood. That was okay, but then he thought it would be cool to see how far he could go with his eyes closed!"

"Do I want to hear this?" Lin asked.

"Probably not! He did alright until he took out someone's mailbox and then landed in a line of aluminum trashcans. Needless to say, that was like an alarm system. Neighbors all came running out from everywhere."

"Did he get hurt?"

"He cut his arm and his ego. The ego took the worst damage. But he jumped back on the bike, now with crooked handlebars, and raced away, trying to avoid being caught. One of the neighbors yelled for him to stop and followed him on foot."

By now, Jenn and Lin were both wiping their eyes at the vision of David as a boy in this situation.

"He knew he couldn't go back to Grandpa's house with this guy in hot pursuit, so David took the longest way possible back to their house. He finally lost the man on his trail and limped back to Grandpa's.

"Luckily, he was able to repair the handlebars, but not the arm. It was bleeding all over the place and Mom had to fix it. I'm sure she suspected something was up, but he gave her a quick "pothole" story.

"Tom and I always wondered if they believed him, but we didn't dare ask. I was afraid of another black eye!" she joked.

"I definitely think he needs to share that story with Uncle Harry. Aunt Martha would have loved it!"

Lin's laughter was replaced with a look of deep thought. "You know, I really never thought about it, but Mother and Aunt Martha should have gotten a gold medal. The only way they had to cook for all that crowd was with an old wood-burning stove, and let me tell you, there was always plenty of food.

"Your grandmother could make better pies and cookies and cinnamon buns than anyone, and she'd spend the entire day in that kitchen over that huge old stove. Sometimes Auntie Larsen, her sister, would come and help, but Mother and Aunt Martha did all the cooking for all those people. Some vacation that was!"

Jenn nodded. "I'm sure she loved every minute of it."

"I'm sure she did, too. What I think was the hardest though, is that they had to heat all the water on that stove and wash the dishes, the clothes, and us in a large pan.

"There were berries galore on the farm, so George and Dave and I picked blueberries and raspberries all summer long and Mother and Aunt Martha would can them and use them in the pies."

The church bells chimed the hour. Lin glanced down at her watch.

"It's that late already? I'd better get back home. It was such a beautiful day that I had to come and enjoy the Green for a while." She gave Jenn a hug. "You be sure and share that with Uncle Harry and George for me."

"I will. Thanks for the stories. I really needed to hear those today."

"My pleasure. It's always a treat to go back to the summers of one's life."

Jenn could hardly believe her ears. Just when she had been thinking about what her grandfather did as a boy, she learned what he did in the summer of his life, and what her father and uncle did in the spring of their lives. *And I was reminded of what my brothers and I did in the transition from the springs to the summers of our lives.*

She thought back over Lin's stories and the old farmhouse and contemplated on whether it was like the farmhouse in Arvika. *No wonder Grandpa loved the Froling Farm so much. He didn't get many days of summer growing up as a boy in Sweden.*

CHAPTER 9

The days, shortening with the approach of fall, had caused the cloudless blue sky to be tinged with a hint of bright pink in the far horizon.

Jenn laughed. *My hat. My Hot Lips hat. The afternoon sky is the same color as my hat.* Jenn made a mental note that she would look for that hat, the same one that had been sliding in and out of her thoughts for the past two days, after picking Sammy up at the Education Center. *It will give her a chance to visit with Gammel Farfar.*

She recalled Pop's statement about "wasting half the day away" if he got up later than six in the morning. *That settles it!* Jenn decided to pick Sammy up early so they could go for a walk in Harrybrook Park and feed the ducks. *Another activity I remember doing with Grandma and Grandpa when I was her age.* She sighed. *And she loves the "duckies" just as much as I did.*

Then we can come back to the Green so she can climb on the tank.

A shudder ran through her body. *Climb on the tank? What am I thinking? I can't allow my child to be climbing and playing on such a monster of destruction.*

Jenn's thoughts stopped as rapidly as if she'd been struck on the head. She looked in the direction of the tank and saw another young mother walking toward it, a small child holding either hand. Her eyes stared at the two little ones as their mother sat one, then the other, on the tank's heavy metal body.

It wasn't but a moment before they were laughing and screaming with glee as they tromped and frolicked from one end of the tank to the other, making up their own little hide-and-seek game as they went.

Jenn took in a deep breath and gave an equally long exhalation. *It isn't the tank that's the monster of destruction. It's man and what he does with it.* Then her mind turned to Pop. *Like our lives. We're all given one and in the end, it's all about what we did with it.*

Comments from friends who knew Pop rushed

through her mind.

"I can't believe his appetite. He still eats as much or more than I do."

"Some people become hunched or shriveled as they grow older. But not this man. Not Harry Kullgren. No, sir. That man is as tall in stature as the day I met him."

"And look at the way he carries himself. It wasn't until a couple of years ago that he began to use a cane and he did it with such style, such grace. Never humped or giving way to it. He commanded that cane with authority, just like he did of himself his entire life."

"That man has more of his faculties than I do and I'm only half his age. Besides the fact that he has a bit of trouble with his eyes and can't read as he once did, the man's the same as he was in his twenties."

"Speaking of 'in his twenties,' have you ever seen the photograph of him in New York City with the singing group from the Swedish Methodist Church on Lexington Avenue and 53rd Street. The one where he was seated in the front row? What a dashing and dapper young man he was. And it was obvious, seeing as how he was surrounded by young women and the other men were standing on the back row, that all those ladies had thoughts of spending time with him."

The comments ... all from people at church, or birthday and anniversary parties, or the number of visitors who had come to call in his later years as he stayed in more. Comments that said that people saw the "real" Harry Nils Kullgren. Comments that said that people saw "inside" Harry Nils Kullgren.

"Comments that said that people saw his attitude and faith in action," Jenn stated aloud.

"Excuse me, I didn't understand you."

Jenn looked up and saw a librarian, walking across the Green, who happened to have heard her. *Not twice in the same week!* Jenn winced. "I guess I was thinking out loud."

The librarian nodded as if she'd done the same at some point in time. "I fully understand." It was then that the woman, a member of New Milford United Methodist Church, recognized the young woman on the bench. "Oh, good afternoon, Jenn. I didn't recognize you at first." Before giving time for a reply, she muttered on, "How's Pop?"

Jenn gave a broad smile. "He's fine. Everything's fine."

"Ah, the same as usual, huh?"

"Yes, the same as usual." The granddaughter's smile grew even larger. "The same as it's been for nearly a hundred and two years."

The librarian nodded in agreement as she

rushed on toward the library. "He's such a dear. You're all lucky to have him," she called behind her.

"Yes, thank you, we are," replied Jenn, her voice tapering off with each word, not sure whether the librarian had heard her, but sure that the response was as much for herself as for the librarian.

More comments ran through her head, none of them critical, and each with an air of amazement and awe at how much life he still possessed and the quality of the life he still had.

"He's like old gunpowder. Strong!" Sture, a Swedish cousin had said.

Gunpowder! Yes, she looked at the tank. *That is exactly like Pop's life. Things can either be used for good or for bad. He's seen the same bad in the world as every-one else, but he chose not to participate. For Pop, he chose the path of the "promised life," and because of it, he's been blessed with a good life. Even in those bad times.*

She could hear him now. "We *lived through it, we made it through, one day at a time, those were the days, I am blessed...,"*

I'm opting for the good life, a life of summer days!

Jenn's attention turned back to the two young tikes on the tank. She quickly reached into her purse for her keys and headed for the van, determined to enjoy the afternoon at Harrybrook Park and with the tank...*and my daughter.*

CHAPTER 10

The Hot Lips hat surfaced from the hall closet, along with Pop's family album. Samantha was as fascinated with the hat as her mother had been years before, and Jenn was enjoying Pop's album as much as he had years before. *And still does*, Jenn noted, watching his face with the turn of each page.

"Exactly how old *were* you and Dad when you began to look different?" Jenn thumbed through the album and saw that, even while they were in high school, college and then both married with children of their own, she could not tell which one was Uncle George and which was her father.

"I think it was about the time we hit mid-life.

You know, that has a way of doing something to you."

Jenn gave a long, discerning stare at her uncle while envisioning her father standing beside him. *Yes, I can see the resemblance in their faces, but there is certainly no difficulty in telling them apart now.*

"Trying to size us up, I see," smiled George.

"Yes. I guess you saw through that stare."

"We get it all the time when we're around other family members or longtime friends. They, too, try to figure out when we lost the 'look alike' contest."

Jenn pulled up a chair from the dining table, scooted it next to Pop's recliner and placed the photo album in his lap. She pointed to the picture of the twins as toddlers. "Can you tell which one is which, Grandpa?"

He pointed to the one on the left. "I think this one's Dave."

She burst into laughter.

"Hey, who started the party without me?" came David's voice from the den as he rounded the corner. "Uncle George!"

The two men embraced as dear friends who had not seen each other in a long while. Jenn loved seeing, and sensing, the way they all related to each other now that she and David were adults with their own children. It was most endearing to watch her uncle, who had once grabbed her and swung her into the air while twirling her about, now do the same thing with her own daughter. *And to see him take Travis fishing nearby as he once did with Tom and David.*

There was a respect factor that had somehow mysteriously developed inside her, without her knowledge, just as had the maturity levels of her physical, mental and emotional being. She had never been cognizant of it. *Until now.* Jenn wondered if David noticed it in himself, too.

"Samantha, come and see what Uncle George and Morfar looked like when they were your age." She showed the picture to her daughter. "Do you know which one is Morfar?"

"Uh-huh," came the excited little voice, and with that Samantha pointed to one of the boys.

The adults all laughed.

"Do you know which one is you?" David asked of his uncle.

"I think I'm the one on the left."

The identity quiz became a great game as the five gathered around Pop's chair and turned the pages.

Pages of life. Pages that tell a story all in themselves. Pages of lost identities and faces. Pages of a long personal journey... Pop's.

"You do know that I was born first," bragged George. "To this day, your father tells everyone that he gave me my first push in life!"

Jenn, as did David, laughed. *I see they both inherited Grandma's sense of humor.* She thought back to the story of the crayons, the hole in the wall and the hose in the kitchen window. *I must tell David it's safe to share his bike story tonight.*

She stood and kissed Pop on the forehead. "I love you, Grandpa!"

"I love you, too!"

The granddaughter was so overcome with emotion that she had to make a quick getaway before the tears arrived. Jenn rushed to the kitchen to heat the pizza that she'd brought so they could spend all their time visiting instead of in the kitchen.

Over an old wood-burning stove! She smiled, thinking she'd outsmarted the tears. *Or with the hose!*

Dinner lightened everyone's emotions as she listened to tales of George and Dave growing up and spending their summers in Michigan on the Froling's Farm. It was fun to hear George's side of the stories and watch how Pop and he played off each other, with one mentioning some tidbit that would trigger a memory and another story from the other.

"I can't believe you were ninety-six and danced at Jenn's wedding," David shook his head. The group had gathered back around Pop's chair and were admiring Jenn's wedding pictures.

"Look at this," pointed Tom, who'd arrived just in time for dinner and a lot of ribbing about his impeccable timing. "I remember the day you had these photos taken. Everyone was unsure how Grandpa would feel the day of the wedding, so you had all these pictures shot two weeks prior to the wedding. And then what happened? Grandpa was the star of the show."

"Yeah, Grandpa," David joined. "You danced with Jenn, and then with your sister, Nancy."

"Look how beautiful they both are." Jenn was glad the lump in her throat had gone unnoticed.

"This is my favorite part." Tom turned the page to find another picture. "All these napkin hats. We kids would have gotten a good thrashing for that, but all the Swedes made hats out of their napkins and put them on their heads."

"An old Swedish tradition," smiled Pop. "White hats at the wedding."

"That's one tradition I love!" Tom laughed, pointing to the photo of David and himself placing their napkin hats on their heads and making faces for the camera.

"Yes, and it's the reason we never use real cloth napkins at parties anymore!" Jenn scowled at her brothers, who had pulled the napkins from the dining room table and were folding them into hats.

"I'm just sorry no one did that at my wedding!" David mocked.

"It's only because all the Swedes showed up at Jenn's wedding," offered Tom.

George laughed at the trio and had visions of Dave, Lin and himself. "Who knows what Pop will do at the next wedding?" laughed George.

"That's right, Grandpa!" Jenn gave Pop a hug. "There will have to be another wedding just to see what you'll do!"

"Yep!" Pop laughed. Then in a voice a little less powerful than when he'd sung at David's wedding, at age ninety, but certainly as heartfelt, he began the opening strains of *The Lord's Prayer*.

Jenn saw from David's face that she was not the only one fighting to hold back tears. The music that came from this man who was nearly 102 was breathtaking. He still had incredible musicianship. He still had a remarkable sense of pitch and it was evident that his sense of rhythm was still a part of his soul.

How Jenn longed for Samantha to know more of this dear man. How she longed for her daughter to dance with him. She forced her mind to halt its hopeful wandering and listen to the song that had been the favorite solo of her grandfather for many decades.

"A-men," Pop finished. As if to put his own seal of approval on the song, he said a soft "Amen" right behind it.

"'Amen' is right, Grandpa," came David's confirmation. "There's no other word appropriate to say after hearing you sing that so beautifully."

Pop blushed slightly and shook his head.

"How can you sing those high notes sitting down?" Jenn questioned.

"I always sang the bass," Pop informed her. "Not like my father, who was a tenor."

"But there were tenor range notes in that song. Those notes go all up and down the scale."

"Yep." He gave the faintest hint of a smile. "I sang that dozens of times in church." The sigh that always came with Pop's recollections made its way between his phrases. "There was another solo that I loved to sing. I've been looking for it in my old hymnbooks, but I can't find it anywhere.

"The minister's wife asked me to sing it when I was a young man in New York City. It was a New Year's song, and she especially requested that I sing it one year for the New Year's service. I felt greatly honored for there were many great singers in the choir.

"It was January of 1932, I remember. The first choir I ever belonged to and it was the first solo I sang in that church. Yep, many years have gone by since." There was another sigh.

"How do you remember that service so clearly, Grandpa?" David's puzzled expression matched his question. "I can't even remember what I was doing five years ago, and that was nearly seventy-five years ago!"

David got no explanation, simply more stories. "The choir director was in a wheelchair. He had a son who played the cello and a daughter who played the violin. He also had several students who played the violin that would play with the choir. There were fifty-two singers in that choir."

Jenn and David stared at each other in utter amazement at their grandfather. Not only had he lived to be a hundred years old, he still had control of all his faculties and could run circles around both of them when it came to calling on his memory.

David pulled his sister aside and whispered, "They say the mind's the first thing to go. I think Grandpa's got a long life ahead of him."

"He's already had a long life ahead of him," she whispered back.

"David, go to my bedroom and look on top of the dresser. There's a photograph there of the choir and string band."

The obedient grandson returned in no time carrying a wide picture that had been taken by a professional photographer, whose name and address were stamped on the back of the print. It was the largest photograph that David had ever seen. Taken in the days of black and white, it showed three rows of singers, with several string players intermingled with them, and the beautiful majestic woodwork of the cathedral styling that encased the pipes of the organ. The choir was exactly as Pop described it. He stood proudly on the back row.

"There were many Swedes living in downtown New York City then, so there were three churches close by for them. There was the Swedish Lutheran Church on 50th Street, the Swedish Methodist Church on 53rd Street and the Swedish Baptist Church on 56th Street.

"When I joined the Methodist Church, I had my letter transferred from Sweden. There was a lady in that church, she was a widow, who gave me a long letter after I sang that solo. She said, 'Don't ever let your voice go silent.'

"I loved to sing."

Pop sat silent for a moment. Both Jenn and

David could see the deep rut of concentration on his brow and knew better than to interrupt his thoughts.

"A Swedish minister once offered to pay for me to attend the conservatory. I didn't go. I was proud and did not want to accept his gracious act of charity. That is a decision I have lived to regret."

"But Grandpa," replied Jenn, "your voice, it has always been so beautiful."

"I'm just an ordinary singer. I sang in the choir all my life, but I'm just an ordinary singer."

"No, Grandpa," David disagreed. "You are no ordinary singer. Your songs are full of love and heartfelt emotion. When you sing, you can actually hear God speaking through your soul."

"Ah, I love to sing," Pop reiterated.

It seemed strange to Jenn that neither of Pop's sons, nor any of his grandchildren, had inherited his natural ability of music.

"The blessing that we say at the table, 'Gute Gud,' we used to sing that years ago. My brother-in-law and I sang together. We spent every Sunday together and every week, we alternated between our house and Helen and Walter's house. Every Sunday, we'd go walking in the late afternoon after supper. Helen was here in America before Martha. They looked like twins when they were together in later years."

This is the same story Lin shared this afternoon, she noted.

Pop stared down at the picture of the singers.

"Did Grandma sing in the choir? Is she in that picture?" Jenn asked.

"No, she didn't sing in the choir." He looked at the other faces in the photograph. "No, she did not."

Jenn wondered if any other people in that photo were still alive.

"The church had a morning service, an afternoon service and an evening service. There were refreshments after the evening service. A couple from Scandinavia invited us over for a cup of coffee one evening. It was like a block party because there were so many Swedes in the area. That was the first time I met Martha. It happened after the church service. I had been in America for maybe two to three years before I met her."

Jenn thought it strange at first that Pop remembered everything about singing in the choir so emphatically, yet was so vague about whether it was two or three years in America before he met her grandmother. Then it struck her. Martha and he had been so much a part of each other, they had been married so long, that there was never a time that, basically, he could remember being without her.

What a beautiful love story! she smiled as she recalled how it was that she finally learned how her grandparents met. Feeling like she was on the park bench again at the Green, her mind wandering from time and place, she vividly recalled that birthday trip to Sweden.

That trip when she'd spent the entire airplane ride trying to find out how they met. That trip when she'd listened for any little tidbit that might give her an inside scoop on their introduction to each other. That trip when the most unlikely of characters was finally the one who gave her the history of her grandparents' initial meeting that led to a sixty-three-year marriage.

It was at the very end of the trip, *the "homecoming,"* the last night they were in Sweden. There was a large birthday party for Pop - *at a church, of course* - with many family members from Sweden joining the ones from the States who had made the trek.

Family members and one long-time friend…the girlfriend who had been left behind in Sweden.

Jenn had found out about her grandparents' meeting from "the girlfriend." *"The girlfriend" who was in her nineties.* She still recalled how odd she'd thought it for such an elderly woman to think of herself, and introduce herself, as "the girlfriend."

"I'm the one he left behind," she had a cousin translate from Swedish into English. "We were to be married. Harry was going to come back in five years with the money he had saved and we were going to build our own house and have our own family in Arvika."

Jenn had hung onto the woman's every word, wishing she'd hurry and finish the tale. But it seemed "the girlfriend" had waited for all these decades to tell the story, and she was going to make it worth the wait. "When the Crash hit in America and the Depression robbed every one of their jobs and money, I learned that my life with Harry was never to be. He found the lady God had given him in America, and thank goodness, he found a good Swedish woman to take good care of him and he of her." The cousin listened intently to every word and then relayed the story a few words behind her.

The elderly woman looked at Pop, a gaze of deep admiration still present in her eyes. "Ah…," Her lone word sounded more like a sigh than a word. "And I found my beloved here in Arvika, and he took good care of me and I of him."

Jenn was amazed that even without knowing and understanding the Swedish language, she could almost guess what the woman was saying, even before the cousin's translation. She looked at Pop, who also sat and listened as if he were hearing this for the first time. *He probably is hearing it for the first time. I'm sure this woman did not share this story with my grandmother.* Later, however, Jenn learned from Pop on the plane home that this woman had indeed introduced herself to Martha when they returned to Sweden in 1969 for the first time in forty years.

At the church in 1999, when the story was over, "the girlfriend" insisted on sitting beside Pop during the dinner at the birthday party. No one bothered to argue with her when she boldly declared, in Swedish, that she had "waited longer than anyone else here to sit beside Harry." In reality, she was right, so they let her sit right there beside him.

And gawk at him the entire time, Jenn now smiled, thinking back on the evening.

She remembered thinking that theirs was a friendship that could not be erased by time and space. What the woman held for her grandfather was a deep respect and admiration, as was shown by the fact that she was grateful that he had found a good woman, "a good Swedish woman," in America to take care of him. She had accepted that it was not a part of God's universal plan that they be betrothed to each other.

Friendships like that are few and far between, she mused while recalling a picture farther back in the album of Pop and the woman at the party. The woman had on a pointed circular party hat, one like a child would wear at a friend's birthday party. Jenn's pleasant smile remained. *They were practically children the last time they saw each other before Grandpa left Arvika. They were younger than I am now.*

Jenn stared at her grandfather, wondering if the admiration on her own face resembled that of the woman that had waited an entire lifetime to celebrate a birthday with this dear friend. Her thoughts of the elderly woman dissipated into thin air as she heard Pop continuing his story of meeting Martha, filling in all the details that "the girlfriend" had left out. *Only because those were the details she didn't know.*

"The Depression was over when I met her," he was saying. "Yes, Martha was in my church. She had a good job. I was a carpenter and had a steady job. We had a wedding in the church.

"They sold the old church where we first met. A skyscraper sits now where the old church stood. They tore it down to build the large building. Our congregation bought two brownstones and tore them down to build a new church on 58th Street. The church is still there, but it is now a Spanish church.

"We got married in 1935. Ours was the first wedding in the new sanctuary. George and Dave were the first babies christened there."

Yes… what a beautiful love story… and to think that it happened after the church service… that they met because of the church… the one thing that had been most important to both of them in their lives. No wonder they had such a long and fulfilling life together. They put their church, or rather, their love for their church, and their love for each other before every thing else in life.

The endearment written all over Pop's face as he talked about the church – the people – and the sanctuary of the church on Lexington Avenue, *or rather, the two churches on Lexington Avenue,* was worth more than any picture of words.

Jenn smiled as she watched him glow, brighter than any sunset she'd ever seen. *He had a beautiful summer.*

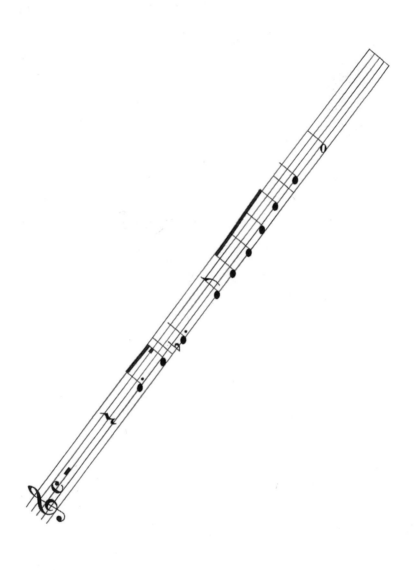

PART THREE

AUTUMN

The preparation for the harshness of winter
when strength and vitality begin to fade
and in its place, a colorful reminder
of all that was

A season of rare beauty
when the pain and memories of life
become as treasures of gold and silver

CHAPTER 11

Thursday

The morning, predicted to be rainy, roared with a rush of the wind and leaves blowing ferociously in every direction, giving their own virtual air show.

Thank God the weatherman missed the mark this morning! The temperature was even warmer than it had been on the previous day.

As Jenn backed out of the garage, on her way to take Samantha to the Education Center, she noticed the pile of leaves that had been tediously raked in her back yard. A huge smile spread across her face as she stopped the van, got out and unfastened the child restraint on the car seat.

"C'mon, Sammy. Want to play a game?"

"Uh-huh," came the excited response from the back seat.

"It was a favorite game of Mommy's when I was a little girl."

Jenn stood her daughter on the ground before taking off toward the leaves, kicking them in every direction as she plowed through them. No invitation was necessary for the young child to come running behind her, laughing gleefully in expectation of strewing her own leaves.

It wasn't long before the neat pile of leaves was a mesh of brown all over the back yard and red little cheeks of a happy glow were on the faces of both the mother and the daughter.

"Do it again!" clapped Samantha. "Do it again, Mommy!"

"Oh, alright," Jenn consented, taking her hands and piling up the leaves again.

The couple tore through the leaves like Jenn had done years before with her brothers. Samantha reached down to help her mother rebuild the pile, but as soon as she got a handful together on the ground, she would immediately run through them, laughing as hard as she could, as if the laughter were a major stipulation of the game.

Thus began the morning that marked Jenn's insight into the autumn of one's life.

It appeared that everyone on the Green had the same idea as Jenn had earlier that morning. All activity revolved around the leaves, from children and dogs playing, to adults saving them, to the city truck vacuuming them with the huge hoses.

Jenn watched as one little boy picked up a leaf and handed it to his baby sister, who immediately placed the leaf in her mouth. *A little Tom or David in the making.*

One of the leafs, the largest one she had seen during the week, fell at Jenn's feet. She picked it up and placed it between the pages of her book as a lasting treasure of her week. Rather than sitting back down to read, she decided to beat the lunch crowd.

Sirens from the volunteer fire department, just around the corner, broke into the peaceful and serene air of the autumn morning. Jenn watched, as suddenly, the blaring horns controlled the action of the citizens and all the goings-on around the Green. Within minutes, cars were at a stand still.

Traffic sure seems to be backed up. Wonder what's going on?

Like the rest of the pedestrians and spectators

along Main Street, her eyes were directed toward Route 7 as she walked toward the Grand Patisserie. Even though it was mild for a fall in New England, the changing colors of the leaves up and down the Green indicated that it was the perfect time for a bowl of freshly prepared New England Clam Chowder and halved slices of warmed and buttered Six-Grain bread, baked from scratch that morning.

She'd heard that description earlier in the week when she'd tried one of their pastries, and decided it sounded too good to pass up.

Kevin O'Neill, a high school classmate of Jenn's who was now one of New Milford's finest, came running out the door of the Grand Patisserie, his right hand across his chest and holding the talk button on his phone as he scrambled for his keys with his left hand. Within seconds, he was in his cruiser and turning right from Main Street onto Route 7, breaking into the rest of the traffic. His siren echoed with screams through the air as he passed between the lanes of two-way traffic.

There must be something big happening down the road. This is most unusual for a late-morning in the fall of this little town.

A chill ran through Jenn as she recalled a cold December morning several years back when she was home from college on Christmas break. She and her mother were taking a stroll up the Green to admire the annual display of Christmas trees. It was the kind of gorgeous evening that belonged on the front of a Currier-and-Ives Christmas card. There was no traffic and people were moving so slowly that one could imagine what Christmases were like a century before, when there were stables for horses behind the houses on the Green.

That was, until someone rushed out of one of the prestigious homes and began to scream that a young woman had just been murdered. Although the murder had taken place in a town thirty miles away, it was a young woman who was preparing to move into an efficiency apartment on the upper floor of a building across the street from the Green.

Suddenly the street was full of residents and shoppers who had come outside to commiserate on such a sad situation for a small town, especially to have happened during the week before the blessed holiday of Christmas. People of every religion gathered on the Green and joined their hearts and hands in a time of silence for the family of the twenty-four-year-old who had lost her life in a violent act.

Jenn remembered how the people were too shocked to be in tears and how there was nothing, except the snow reflecting the lights of the trees and the candles in residents' windows, to illuminate the evening air. A soft gentle snow began to fall as if they were frozen droplets of sorrow from God for what had happened to one of His children. No one said a word as people returned to their homes, shoppers got in their cars and drove away and shopkeepers turned out the lights and turned the store signs to read "Closed."

The joy that had been in the air only moments earlier had turned to a sickening mournful feeling that spread to the souls of all who had been a part of the circle of prayer and sympathy.

I hope this is not another catastrophe like that!

"Someone cut into a gas line down near the bridge. The road's closed all the way from the bridge to the McDonald's on the other side of town." A man stood on the sidewalk shouting what he had over-heard from Kevin's walkie-talkie as the officer had run toward his car. The man's stance and voice her-alded a pride in being the town crier for the event.

I wonder if this is how it was all those years ago when there really was a town crier in the streets of the small New England villages, Jenn mused as she watched the reaction on passersby's faces and in their voices.

"My wife just called," yelled another man, who came running out of the corner drug store. "Says they're evacuating everyone within two miles of the incident on Bridge Street in every direction. A gas truck just blew up and there's been a big explosion!"

Gasps filled the air and people, trying to get home to loved ones as quickly as possible, rushed for their cars.

Seems all the recent natural disasters have people in a scramble. Jenn, trying to control her senses and emotions, decided to take a hike down Bank Street to see if her mother, at the newspaper office, knew the real scoop.

It turned out that the man who'd heard the one-sided conversation coming through Kevin's radio was closest to the truth. People were asked to stay away from the area to allow trucks and repairmen from the gas company the necessary space and passage to get the west side of town back to normal. An employee at a gas station near the bridge, in his effort to get rid of the last remnants of the prior week's flood, had accidentally hit a gas line supplying the station.

Shows what happens when people panic before they have all the truth. She walked back up Bank Street and made a left turn back toward Grand Patisserie and her bowl of chowder. *The effect the media has had on the public with all the recent disasters.*

Jenn was looking forward to Lindley's return from his photo shoot, with the birds-eye story of the damages from the Gulf Coast and how to best help the families left in the areas struck by the recent floods and hurricanes.

As she sat at a small table at the front window, savoring every bite of the delicious chowder, she listened to the increasing exaggerations of the morning's event from customers. Rather than get involved, Jenn left them to their own devises of believing what they wished. She also made a promise to herself to take things as they came, one step at a time, before letting herself get caught up in unnecessary and stressful panic.

One step at a time. The five-word phrase slipped without warning. *The five words that usually follow "One day at a time."*

One day at a time. One step at a time. They both mean the same. Perhaps all those times of Grandpa uttering those words every time something happened made an impact on us grandkids after all.

As she took slow, deliberate spoonfuls of the chowder, she reflected on her grandfather's life in relationship to the fall that now painted New Milford, and especially the Green. The pace of life seemed to move a bit slower, as even the cars didn't rush quite as hurriedly as usual. The year was winding down to a close. Yet creation caused everything around it to halt and take notice of the beauty it possessed in these final days before the closing of a season, and the moving on to a quiet winter that prepared all of earth and humanity for a new beginning, a new season.

The splendor of the golds and deep reds, with the sun shining down on them in full radiance, gave the leaves a majestic, regal appearance. Much like the regality that one's life possessed by surviving so many historical events - *and natural disasters* – that "knighted" one with a wisdom that only came with years of knowledge through experience. *The beauty of one's life,* Jenn surmised, trying to use the earned wisdom of her own youthful years. *That's what the autumn of one's life is.*

A streak of sadness rippled through her at the number of young people who were missing out on the beauty and wisdom of their grandparents, either through distance, or worse, their rebellious years of indifference. For the first time in her life, the dynamic of how blessed she was to know, and have known, her grandparents struck her.

Even in her teenage years, her grandmother and grandfather had blessed her life. *And how you blessed theirs*, she seemed to hear in the distance, as if the message were riding on a leaf that gently glided through the air past the bakery cafe's front door.

She thought of other family members and friends who were also in the autumn of their lives.

Some of them had ailments or chronic illnesses, and many didn't move with the spryness of step that they once had. But she had seen and heard the beauty still radiated by many of them, and their stories of life.

Autumn. The beauty of one's life. Jenn said the words over several times in her mind. *Yes, that's a suitable analogy.*

I wonder when the autumn of Pop's life began. She thought of the many stories she'd heard that happened long before she was born. Finally, she decided that season of his life must have begun one day in 1969. *The day of his retirement.*

Pop had worked long and hard his entire life, holding fast to his philosophy of eight hours of work for eight hours of pay. "And making those around him do the same," she'd heard more than once from other family members. But when it came time for him to retire at age sixty-five, one summer day in 1969, he laid down his hammer and went home.

How many times she'd heard the recounting of that story. "You can't do that!" the boss at the United Nations Building yelled behind him. "I still have more work for you to do."

"Oh, yes, I can," replied Pop, the general foreman for the carpentry repairs, without looking back. He kept walking at the purposeful speed he had maintained his whole life, grabbed his hat and coat off the rack on his way out the door, and walked down the street toward the train station for the very last time.

Yes, Jenn felt confidently, *that was definitely the day his autumn began.*

She took the last bite of chowder, making it last as long as possible, as if there were some related symbolism between drawing out that last bite, and humanity drawing out the last bite of life and vitality. *Like the leaves outside that swirl and dance in rhythm, giving their grandest of displays, before giving up that life of being in the air - on top of things.*

She glared out the front window, reflecting on the autumns of her grandfather's past - those years she had known him. That's when it dawned on her that she had only known him since the autumn of his life; that she had first-handedly witnessed the beauty of his life. *And it was truly richer and more glorious than the show of the leaves I've watched this week - even in their majesty of royal colors.*

But now, Grandpa's moved on to the winter of life. Jenn wiped her mouth with the thick napkin. *Yes, I'd say that anything over one hundred years definitely qualifies one for the winter of life.*

She paid the bill and returned, book in hand, to "the" bench. As she passed another bench on the way to her designated spot, Jenn overheard two women talking about a dam in Massachusetts that had taken a hard hit from the past week's flood.

"You know, that's only an hour away from here. I wonder how far that water can travel."

"Relax, dear. They've evacuated all the people that they think are in harm's way. Besides, no one is even sure that the dam will go."

"Well, you know as well as I do, that dam is only made of wood, and it's a hundred years old. There's no way that structure can hold up against the might of those rushing waters."

"I wouldn't worry so if I were you. Just because that dam is over a hundred years old doesn't mean that it doesn't still have some life left. You know how old many of those dams and bridges are in Europe. They were built sturdy to start with. They were meant to last."

Yeah, like Grandpa, thought Jenn, biting her tongue to keep from adding her own comment. *He came from strong Swedish stock. He was built to last. He's over one hundred and he still has plenty of life left in him.* Her favorite comment about her grandfather, the one made by her cousin, Sture, in Sweden came to mind for the second time this week. She could still hear his heavy, thick accent as he said, "Harry is strong, like old gunpowder." How she loved that!

Before she had time to verbalize her opinion,

the second woman continued, "Besides, if there was any danger that you could be affected, I'm sure the New Milford police would be knocking at your door to warn you to evacuate."

"But they're all busy with that gigantic gas explosion down at the bridge. See, that proves my point. The bridge is gone. That water can burst that dam and come roaring down the Housatonic and with our bridge gone, it can wipe out the whole of New Milford."

Jenn didn't wait to hear the response to that one. This simply proved her point that people were going to believe what they wished.

She opened her book. *And,* she concluded, *that they should take life one day at a time, with one step at a time.*

CHAPTER 12

The church bells rang thirty-one times. Jenn knew the old story of how the bells from the three churches on the Green were timed to ring, one after the other, so that they never interfered with each other. She also knew that, generations before, signals had been created for the bells' rings to alert the townspeople of various situations.

Musical smoke signals! she grinned.

But thirty-one bells? What kind of signal is that? Jenn glanced at her watch. *Ah, a signal that it's time to pick up Samantha.*

As Jenn crept along, following the cavalcade of cars lined up for a couple of miles in front of her, she saw that her carefully calculated schedule for picking up Samantha at the Education Center was not quite "carefully calculated" enough.

She gave the command for her phone to call the church's number. "Hello, this is Jenn McCaughan. I'm going to be late…,"

Before she had time to continue, the church's secretary interrupted, "Not to worry, Jenn. Everyone else is in the same boat."

"Boat?" Jenn wanted to reply. *"No, the boat was last week, during all the rains and flooding!"* But she kept her grandmother's inherited humor to herself and simply hung up the phone, gratified that her daughter had such positive role models. The problem at hand was settled, but then she was faced with another dilemma. *How am I ever going to have time to go grocery shopping, fix dinner and be ready for Lindley to come home?*

The ringing of the cell phone broke into her bout of stress-inducing questions. *"Great!"* she mumbled. *"Why can't I have lived in the days, like Pop, before cell phones? He obviously did just fine without them."*

Wishing she could ignore the annoying beep, she glanced down at the caller ID before answering. *Uncle George? Oh, no! Something must be wrong.* Her complaint regarding the inconvenience of cell phones immediately vanished.

"Jenn?"

"Uncle George? Nothing's wrong, is it?"

A light chuckle, sounding like her dad's, came through the line. "Not unless you call an invitation to grilled salmon for dinner a bad thing."

"Oh… oh… no… that's not a bad thing at all." She paused. "Well, except that Lindley is supposed to be home…,"

"Relax," he interjected. "There's plenty for everyone. Remember, you come from a long line of Swedes. We invented the smorgasbord."

This time it was Jenn's turn to chuckle.

"Okay, if you're absolutely sure it won't be an imposition."

"Imposition? Are you kidding? The reasoning behind the smorgasbord is 'the more, the merrier.'"

"There's only one problem. What time did you want to eat? I'm stuck in traffic at the moment."

"So I figured. I heard the news with the report of the gas leak. Why don't you just come by after you pick up Samantha? I'll wait to throw the salmon on the grill until you get here."

"Thanks, Uncle George. I'll call Lindley and tell him to come straight there from the airport."

"Great. See you in a bit."

Jenn hung up the phone, her thoughts on her uncle's peaceful, calming voice. *Like that of Pop's.*

There was a certain ease about it, something akin to a sacred rhythm, that exuded a sense of tranquility to whomever he was speaking.

She let her mind wander back to her days of growing up with her father. Now that she thought about it, that same calming voice was a quality that he, too, possessed.

Isn't it odd that I lived with him for over twenty years and just noticed that? And even now, it took my father's identical twin, that's not so identical anymore, *to teach me that lesson.*

She looked to the left of the road at Lake Lillinonah, flowing calmly and peacefully once again after the rush of the flooding waters earlier in the week. *Seems this entire week is turning into one long lesson of the things I should have picked up on during my life.*

Jenn, still in her young adult years, began to feel like an icon of maturity. *My God... and God of my fathers, help me to, like those fathers, remember that You have laid the path out before me. Guide my steps, one at a time, down that path so that I, too, may understand and recognize the rich and miraculous quality of life that comes with taking one day at a time. May I continually remember that, like great riches on earth, those riches are built little by little, sometimes fluctuating up and down - just like our good days and our bad days - but if we keep them stored with You, we will have abundant wealth and treasures.*

"Did you and grandmother know you were going to have twins?" Jenn's question prompted the after-dinner conversation that, as the evening before, revolved around the family album.

The family album... Grandpa's visual record, his bank statement, of abundant wealth and treasure. The moment that thought materialized, another followed behind it of how much families around the world were missing by being tuned in to the television or internet. They were missing life.

Real life. And they call those TV shows "reality?" This is where it's at.

A pang of sorrow ran through Jenn as she visualized the number of people in America sitting in front of some screen or monitor, robbing themselves of the beauty of what life was all about. Robbing themselves of family. *People my age. People Uncle George's age.* She looked at Samantha sitting on Pop's lap and telling him a story from her little book. *And people Samantha's age.*

All the current events of the media came

crashing down on Jenn. *Were these same distractions going on in Pop's youth? Were there bad people that he had to contend with?* Those were questions with which she had struggled all week.

It was the remembrance of Pop's stories that answered those and many other questions shooting through her head. *There were bad people from the very beginning of time. Pop had to deal with them at every phase, every season, of his life.* She paused to reflect on her immediate family and the relatives she had around the world. She contemplated on the many people who had walked through those doors of the United Nations Building with the responsibility of making a world-changing decision. *Everyone's had to deal with them all through life.*

Her heart was tinged again with pain, this time due to the fact that more people didn't have a beautiful heritage and family album with which to spend evenings together. Jenn's eyes were fixed on Pop and Samantha. She fought her own flood, a flood of tears, as she said a hearty prayer of thanks for the lives her family had been given. She also said a prayer for all those who had missed out on the heartening stories of their family's past, that they could begin their own "family album." A family album that would be left for future generations.

"There's always the Bible." Jenn's prayer was

cut short by the words she thought had come from her grandfather. *But he's telling about the birth of the twins. He couldn't have said that.*

She recalled her question that had begun this conversation, barely in time to hear Pop's answer.

"The doctor suspected. He thought he heard two heartbeats."

The doctor suspected! Just as I suspected that I heard those words from Grandpa a moment ago. Jenn contemplated, both on what she heard and what she thought she'd heard, for a brief moment. *That's it! The doctor suspected because he heard life from inside.*

I suspected I heard that phrase from my grandfather and I did. His example of faith is so strong and alive that I did hear those words from him. From his soul, from his heart. Just as the doctor heard the gift of life in my grandmother!

Her focus turned entirely on her grandfather and the rest of the story.

"I was at work when they were born. I had been working downtown at the City Hall that day and when I came home that afternoon, as I was walking up the street, people were shouting, 'Harry! Harry!

"I dropped everything in my hands and took off. Martha's sister had taken her to the hospital. She had to stay almost ten days, but that was in 1941."

"What did you do during World War II?" Jenn

realized she had tons of questions about the life and times of Harry Kullgren, and she intended to find out all the answers.

"I was working on a store on 14th Street in New York City when the war broke out. They were continually updating and having me to build new displays. But I got sent to Texas for a while to do a job with air conditioning using metal. Most of the metal back then was being used for the war effort.

"Then I had to build minesweepers at a place in the North Bronx. The minesweepers all had to be made out of wood. They were going to throw away the scrap lumber from the minesweepers, so I asked if I could take it home. I filled our basement with the spare pieces of lumber. It was our only firewood, but I carried it home every day, so we had enough to last us for two years."

"When we found out the war was over, people were out in the street dancing. Everyone had a good time." Pop gave a slight shake of his head. "That was many years ago." He said that after nearly every story, giving a "The End" effect.

Jenn loved the emotion in her grandfather's eyes. It was apparent from his expressions that he was reliving each story with the telling of it.

"Did you ever think you'd see a man walk on the moon, Grandpa?"

Pop didn't bat an eye. "No!" His voice dropped with the exclamation, silently admitting that he'd never even *thought* of seeing a man walk on the moon. "It happened while we were on our trip to Sweden. Martha and I were leaving Copenhagen and there was a special announcement that came over the loud speakers. They said, 'Americans just landed on the moon!' There were gasps all over the airplane."

The mention of that first return to Sweden started Pop telling his most cherished moments from the trip. "I'll never forget standing on the deck as we were approaching Norway. I didn't want to miss a thing. All of a sudden, I heard a male voice yelling, 'Harry! Harry!'" I looked in the direction of the voice and it was my brother Eric. All my family was there, waiting and watching for us. They recognized me. I was so excited to see them.

"When the ship docked, we were able to go ashore for a bit, but then we had to get back on board to take our meals. It was a very nice boat and we ate all three meals a day on it. I told the crew about leaving Sweden and my family meeting me at the dock. They allowed me to bring thirteen family members to dinner, and didn't charge me any extra. They sat us all upstairs together and said, 'Enjoy!' Pop's face lit up like the trees on the Green at Christmas. "And we did!"

Jenn picked up the family album, turning to the where she'd left off the evening before. She leafed through the book, page after page with each one evoking an explanation from Pop, until she came upon a faded and yellowed newspaper. It was the front page of a Swedish newspaper with Pop's visit, after forty years, as the headline. She couldn't read the words, but she gathered the gist of the article from the expressions, written on the faces in the photo with him, that it was a happy time.

"You're a celebrity, Pop!"

He gave a hearty laugh. "Nope."

"Oh, yes, you are, Pop," insisted Jenn. "At least in my book!"

She pulled out an entire manila envelope full of cards, letters and birthday wishes from his past few birthdays. "Look at all these. From the looks of all this, I'd say you're a celebrity in the books of a lot of people!"

And in the most important book of all. God's book! Jenn concluded.

The chord that struck her in all the pictures is that they were of family. No sights of the world, no amusement parks, all family. And most of them were pictures of Martha and Pop with their family.

Except for a few, Jenn noted. *And those are with his choir... still his family.*

"Did you always like to sing, Grandpa?"

"Always!" The caress that was present in that one word said everything Jenn needed to hear. She could imagine her grandfather walking across the Brooklyn Bridge, all the way up Lexington Avenue to 126th Street, looking for work during the Depression. *Singing.* She could see him when there was no work to be found because all the doors were "locked up." *Singing.* She could see him when he had to cut his living expenses, which were $10.00 per week for a boarding house room and three meals a day, to no meals. *Singing.*

Pop's words broke into Jenn's thought bubble. "Anyway, time went on, I lived day by day."

She had missed the words preceding that statement, but she knew they didn't matter. Whatever they were, the outcome was always the same. Pop dealt with it.

"When we had the big revival with the three churches, the one at the synagogue, I was chosen to warm up all the singers and to tune all the instruments. I had to be there an hour early. I sang so much that I abused my voice. I could not sing for a whole year. I was fearful I had destroyed my voice. But...,"

There's his long pause after the word, "but," when you can tell he's seeing the scene in his eyes, Jenn heard.

"One day it came back and I've been able to

sing ever since." He paused with a long reflective sigh. "I love music."

There was silence for several minutes. Pop closed his eyes and Jenn began to wonder if he had fallen into a light slumber. But then, she saw a spark of life on his face. A spark that said he was simply listening to all the songs he had sung. To all the music which had been such an integral part of his life.

To the songs he was singing as he walked over Brooklyn Bridge, as he married grandmother, as he rode to the hospital to see his two sons...

When his eyes opened, Jenn saw into a long tunnel of memories - both good and bad - but all lessons and all cherished parts of life.

"Grandpa, is there anything that you would have done differently?"

"Yes. I would have gone to the conversatory when the minister offered to pay for it, for I now know he meant the offer as a gift to others, not charity for me."

A hint of a smile crossed his lips. "And I would have gone to the classes to learn English. I went a couple of times, but I didn't like it because of where I had to go.

"When sound first came to the movies, there were two movie houses. One on one side of the street and one on the other. It was either five or ten cents to get in, and I went there to learn to speak English. The movies are how I learned the English language."

Jenn laughed at first. It was hard to imagine her grandfather sitting in the movies to learn how to speak. She suddenly shuddered. *What if Samantha had to learn how to speak from the movies?*

She glanced into the adjoining room at her daughter, comfortably cradled in Uncle George's lap, with her pile of books. *Learning English. Learning new words.*

Jenn grabbed her digital camera and made a picture. *Pop's latest addition to his abundant wealth.*

CHAPTER 13

*H*as *this been here all week?*

Jenn stood in front of the Focal Point, a unique gift shop on Bank Street beside Baileywick Books, with her feet firmly planted as she stared in the front window. An object next to the glass screamed at her as she passed on her way to the coffee shop, the same path she'd taken every morning that week. Yet, she was sure that what she saw staring back at her had not been there before.

Or was it here, and I was so busy running and trying to control every minute of my day that I neglected to see it?

She looked at the sign on the door to see what

time the shop opened. A quick glance at her watch revealed that she had precisely enough time to order a latte, sip it relaxingly while reading the *Greater New Milford Spectrum*, and buy the object on her way to her "assigned bench" on the Green.

"What'll it be today?" asked the young man behind the counter.

Jenn nearly laughed aloud. The manner in which he phrased the question, along with his choice of words, made her feel like some cowboy in an old Spaghetti Western, stepping up to the bar, instead of a young woman stepping up to the counter of the Bank Street Coffee House.

She was tempted to say, "The usual," but she had not repeated the same flavor all week. Each morning she had tried the day's house specialty, but today she decided to end the same way she began. "I'll have a Banks Street Crunch."

"You got it."

Jenn felt like a regular, receiving nods from those who had noticed her making their spot hers during the course of the week. As much as she had enjoyed the past week's freedom, and the discovery of a lot of new things about life - or things she had dismissed in her attempt to play "adult" - she found herself welcoming the opportunity to return to her job come Monday.

The cover of the weekly newspaper showed a color photo of the Green, taken two days earlier, of a tree in front of St. John's Episcopal Church, it's stately gray stones a stark contrast to the bright oranges and reds of the tree's leaves. *I shall cut this out and save it when I get home. Who knows when I might need to pull it out as a reminder of this week? I can say, "I remember that. I was there."*

Jenn knew she would relish the photo, and would use it anytime she began to regress into that mode of trying to play the control freak. She tried not to eavesdrop, but she couldn't help but hear the scattered conversations of the regulars around her. Together, they sounded like nothing but gibberish, but individually, they rang with the sounds of life, some happy tones, some sad, but all, *like Grandpa's*, a part of the composition of someone's life story.

She wondered how many of the regulars would tear out the door and rush off to a job, losing all they had gained in that slow-paced, aromatically pleasing environment. *But since I'm not in charge, that's not for me to consider.* She finished the creamy pecan-flavored beverage, folded the newspaper – making sure not to bend the photo of New England's fall foliage – and retraced her steps to the Focal Point.

Still there. Jenn pushed the glass door open, causing a small bell to jingle, and heard a woman in the back say, "Welcome. Make yourself at home and look around."

Jenn followed the voice. "There's something in the front window I'd like to see."

"Not a problem. Just let me finish this ticket I'm working on and I'll be right there."

The owner of the shop hastily made her way to the front of the store. "What may I help you with?"

"This," Jenn pointed. "This little sign here in the front window."

The owner reached through the maze of other decorative objects to an elongated metal base bearing short cut-out letters of the phrase, "ONE DAY AT A TIME."

So I wasn't dreaming, Jenn grinned as the owner placed the sign in her hand. She ran her fingers along the edges of the words, as if at any minute they were going to change shapes and say something entirely different.

There was a slight bend in one of the letters, giving it a defective appearance. *Hmmm... a little less than perfect.* Jenn noted its similarity to humans.

The shop's owner caught Jenn's gaze on the flawed letter. "Here, we can fix that. I have a pair of pliers that will pull that right back into shape."

Jenn smiled and shook her head. "No...I think I want it just the way it is. There's something about this that says no matter what comes, we can get through it if we take it one day at a time. Sort of like a visual reminder that the sign is true in what it says." Jenn sighed and nodded. "Like God can take His pliers, pull out whatever gets in the way of our days, and straighten up our lives."

"I'd have never thought of it that way, but I guess you have a point."

"Yep," Jenn replied, unconsciously mimicking the affirmation she'd heard from her grandfather for years, "a focal point."

The Focal Point's owner smiled appreciatively, considering Jenn's play on words a great compliment.

Jenn handed the sign to the store's owner. "I'd like to buy it."

"Very well. Let me wrap it for you."

"No need. It's for me and I'm going to put it in a highly visible spot once I get home." Jenn took some money from her wallet. "Has this been sitting in the window all week?"

"It surely has. As a matter of fact, it's been here since the spring. They all sold and I guess this one got hidden there. Must have had your name on it."

"Hmmm," was the only response Jenn could manage. *Must have had today's date on it, too!* She exited the shop, bag in hand, carrying the assurance that this day was going to be full of special blessings, rewards that had come from a week of taking things "one day at a time."

My special blessing to myself is going to be a treat to Scotch eggs at Mother's on the Green. No telling when I'll get a chance to have those again. She made the left off Bank Street and strolled past the few facades on the way to the small restaurant, which was basically a narrow path with tables down each side.

As she sat down, she wondered how long this space had been a restaurant. The tables were so close that one could speak to people at the other tables without raising a voice. It still had the charm of the tiny village New Milford had started out to be. She envisioned what it must have looked like two centuries before, with children playing on the Green while mothers stayed indoors and did their housework, and with all the horses and carriages going up and down a dirt path for Main Street.

"No need for a menu," she told the host. "I knew what I wanted before I came through the front door."

"Most of our customers do," the man replied as he took the few steps back to his wooden stand.

"Hello, dear," Jenn heard from a couple of tables back.

She didn't even have to turn around. That voice, with the word "dear" as a part of the greeting, was as familiar to everyone in town as the vision of its owner driving down the street in her PT Cruiser. Jenn wheeled around to see this icon of the town, known to many as the "Queen Mother," due to her poised appearance, and her stately mannerisms and speech. Before she had time to respond, Libby Porter continued.

"Would you like to join me this morning?"

Jenn didn't even answer. She simply slid from her table to Libby's. "Hope I'm not messing you up," she apologized to the waitress behind her.

"Not at all. We're so used to customers joining friends once they get here that we actually expect it. What would you like today?"

"Scotch eggs."

"My favorite," Libby commented. "That's what I'm having, too, dear. Tell me, how is your grandfather?"

Jenn laughed. No one ever asked, "How are you today, Mrs. McCaughan?" It was always, "How is your grandfather?" But she found it humorous, not upsetting, for it showed he had made an impression on many people during his lifetime. She secretly hoped that one day Samantha's children would be hearing, "And how is your dear grandmother?"

"He's fine, Mrs. Porter."

"Call me Libby, dear."

Jenn nodded. "I've been able to spend more time with him than usual this week. Because of the flood, I've had a little time off from the Golf Club."

"Yes, I'd imagine you have. I've not seen the likes of that flood since 1955, just over fifty years ago."

The young mother was fascinated by the stories that poured from the woman across the table. Libby Porter had been in New Milford her entire life – "except the three weeks my mother spent in a Port Jarvis, New York hospital when I was born" - and she recalled every single detail of her life as if it had happened the day before.

"Wasn't that a different day?" Libby asked. "Three weeks indeed! "

The woman gave Jenn a historical insight on many of the buildings on the Green, including the New Milford Congregational Church, of which she was a member.

"We had assigned pews when I was a child. I remember we sat on Pew Number 7. I couldn't wait until I was old enough to sit where I wanted."

Jenn laughed. Although most churches didn't claim to have assigned pews, most of them did, by virtue of where the members sat. She'd sat on the same pew her entire life, too.

It was a highly known fact among the town that Libby was a graduate of the prestigious Russell

Sage College in New York. After a successful career in insurance, she was still actively involved in all the alumni affairs.

"There were 132 in my graduating class. Sixty-three are gone, and there were only 7 of us at our recent 65th reunion. At this age, they roll out the red carpet for us."

Jenn adored listening to this woman. Having grown up in the area, she gave the past an entirely different perception.

"It was during the Depression. I had three jobs on campus, but it was worth it." Libby shared the story of how her mother, a nurse, took in patients who had no family to care for them. "She was really ahead of her time. She was determined that I would have a college education so that if anything happened, I could take care of myself."

Jenn knew that Libby had served on the VNA, Visiting Nurse Association, of which nurses came to check on Pop from time to time. She wondered if her interest in the organization had passed from her mother.

"Yes, I served on that board for 54 years," Libby confirmed. "Did you know it was founded in 1918 during the flu epidemic?"

During breakfast, Jenn learned all about the founding of the hospital and the VNA.

"My mother loved caring for others. She had someone in our home, even in the 80's.

"In all of those years, though, her family came first and foremost. Yes, dear, she'd have us on Pew Number 7, keeping us quiet and our hands folded in our laps."

As the two women exited the restaurant, each headed their own way, Jenn thought of a photo of her father, her grandfather, Libby and Axel Karlsson - another dear family friend - in the bandstand. She recalled the Saturday, only months earlier, that photo had been taken. It was a gorgeous summer morning, complete with a perfect sky.

When she and her dad arrived with Pop, the photographer informed him that he didn't have to climb the steps, that a ground shot should work.

"I can make it!" Pop enthusiastically replied. He climbed the steps and took his place among the foursome.

He *had* made it. So had Libby. So had a good number of others in the autumn of their life.

The photo shoot ended with a trip to Clamp's - the small hamburger stand that was just as it had been at its birth in 1939. *Another place that made it!* Jenn reflected as she rode with her father and grandfather, to the tiny spot eight miles out of New Milford.

She silently laughed at the thought of it, for

the opening of Clamp's was the way many locals could tell when when summer was near. All it took was one person to see the roadside joint open, and the word spread like wildfire throughout the land.

The hamburger stand had been the focus of several food magazines and internet sites. People would line the street for their turn in line, and for a seat at one of the outdoor tables, made from old spools that had once held telephone cable.

That summer day ended with four generations of Kullgren's seated on the Green, their lawn chairs in front of the bandstand, listening to one of the weekly summer serenades.

And Jenn's last day of her week off ended with her seated on a bench, near that same spot, listening to the serenade of life.

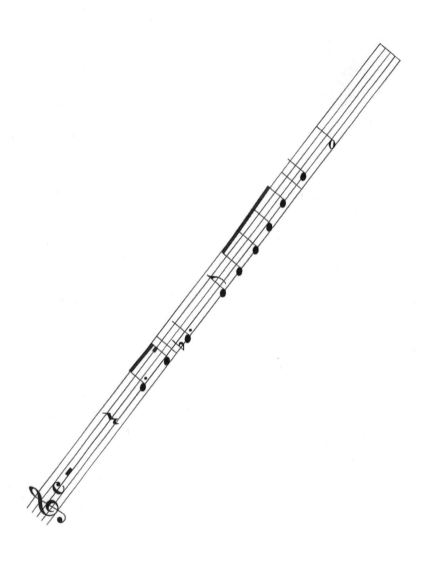

PART FOUR

WINTER

A world of white
when a blanket of snow covers the earth
protecting it from the harshness of nature

When hair has turned to silver or white
and one's wisdom blankets those he loves
like a protective shield
against an unknown future

CHAPTER 14

November

M ommy... Mommy!"

Samantha was awake earlier than usual. Jenn had purposely put her daughter to bed early the night before in hopes that she'd wake up, as was her usual schedule, after ten hours of sleep. Like clockwork, the young child was calling for her mother at exactly the same time the alarm went off in the master bedroom.

"What's the occasion?" Lindley asked, rolling over in bed and noticing the extraordinarily early hour for the clock to sound on a Saturday morning.

"This is the day they put up the Christmas trees on the Green. I've decided that Samantha needs to see this. It's a tradition that her "Morfar" has been involved with since I was Samantha's age."

"You have to go this time of morning to see them? Doesn't it take a while to do all that work?"

"Yes, it does, but Samantha and I are going to have Scotch eggs at Mother's on the Green while we wait for the adventure to start. I'm hoping we can get the front corner table by the window so she can watch it from somewhere warm."

"Good idea!"

"And you should come down and take a few photos, Mr. Photographer."

Lindley managed half a smile as he turned his head back over and buried it on the pillow. "Maybe I will." He shuffled the covers until he found his comfortable spot again. "Maybe I will... later... much later."

Jenn had the child up and dressed in no time. "Ready for Mommy's and Samantha's special day?"

Samantha's outstretched hands indicated that she was ready to go. The youngster had no idea where she was going or what she was going to do when she got there, but she could tell by her mother's voice that this was one engagement she did not want to miss.

Jenn had eagerly anticipated this day ever since her week on the Green when she realized what a great experience it was for a child to grow up in New Milford. This was one of those annual traditions that a child could look forward to every year. *How many years did I come to see the trees going on up the Green?* she questioned herself, buckling Samantha into the car seat.

There was a heavy frost in the morning air, indicating that nature was certainly cooperating with the delivery of a perfect day for putting up the trees. It was cold, very cold, but it was warmer than some of the past years. *And thankfully,* Jenn noticed as she drove toward the center of town, *there's no rain in sight for today.*

During the course of years she'd been privy to this annual tradition, she had seen rain, snow and hail – anything that Mother Nature had to offer. On a scale of 1 – 10, this was about as good as it got for outdoor work in the winter of western Connecticut.

She whipped into a parking spot right in front of the restaurant just as the clock chimed the hour. *8:00? Good, the men should be arriving soon.*

As hoped, the owner allowed Jenn to occupy the front table with Samantha, even though it was meant to hold a larger group of people. The host, who had never seen the trees and the lights go up, was as excited as Jenn and Samantha.

Jenn had explained the entire process to her daughter on the way to the restaurant, sufficiently enough that the child was standing in the booth, her hands on the glass, watching for any sign that the show was about to begin.

It wasn't long until, one by one, the men arrived like a caravan, most of them in trucks loaded with trees, or the large plastic containers of supplies necessary for holding the trees tall against the sometimes 60 mph winds that ripped through the Green.

"I wonder how many trees there are?" asked the restaurant's host.

"Seventeen," answered Jenn. She didn't move her attention from the window.

Samantha stood, her hands and face pressed against the glass as, with the trees, her fascination mounted. "Morfar, Morfar," she belted, her feet stomping up and down on the bench when she spotted her grandfather parking his car in one of the spots in front of the library.

Dave walked briskly back to the side of a truck parked near the Green's military tank as another man helped him to drag a tree out of the back of the truck and across the ground to where it would stand. The truck pulled forward a few yards and the process was repeated. Like rhythmical clockwork, the men followed this procedure for three trees. That truck would be emptied and another would pull into the circular drive of the Green, right on cue, for the two men to pull another tree to a spot where it would hold great prominence for the next few weeks.

"How long do the trees stay up?" inquired the host.

"That depends on the weather. Some years there's so much snow they have to wait until spring to even get the trees up out of the ground. I can remember years that they'd come to remove the lights after Christmas and the strands would be completely frozen to the branches from the cold and snow."

The man gave a chuckle. "Why don't they just leave them up and decorate them with spring colors and stuffed bunnies for Easter?"

Jenn smiled. "Now there's a thought. I'll share that with my dad." She turned toward Samantha. "How do you like the Scotch eggs?"

The child, who normally had a good appetite, had to be reminded to take bites of her food. For the moment, she had found something more fulfilling than food. Samantha leaned down, picked up a piece of the sausage and egg with her fork, crammed them in her mouth and immediately stood back upright to continue to watch all the action on the Green.

The second round of trucks each had a man walking along beside them, pulling out wooden boxes with rope handles which held the iron pipes used for supporting the trees, and large garbage containers of stakes and wire to hold the trees in place. A third round of trucks had two men beside them, one pulling out large garbage containers of the strands of lights, and another man pulling out a large plastic bin that held replacement bulbs.

Men lined the Green, some carrying ladders, some hammers, some plastic tote bins full of bundles of electrical cords. They processed in such a regal and rhythmic manner that they resembled the Three Wise Men bearing gifts.

A gift indeed, mused Jenn. *A gift for the entire community of New Milford.* "Nothing's changed in years," she shared with the host, who was now seated behind Samantha and watching as enthusiastically as the child. "They put the trees up today, then they light them the Saturday after Thanksgiving.

"See the light bulbs?" She didn't stop to catch his answer. "Those are the olde-timey kind they've used for years. Red, blue, green, yellow and white."

For the first time in her own life, Jenn made the connection between those light bulbs, the tradition of these trees and what they said. *It's a lot more than simply a line of trees with shining lights for a month or so out of every year. It's all about community. It's all about life. It's all about the seasons of nature and one's life.*

She felt a tear trickle down her cheek. *And it's all about how blessed I am to have been raised here, and to be able to raise my own daughter here in a place that hasn't forgotten those days of a time gone by. Days when New Milford was still a village and the people were what mattered.*

Jenn noticed Samantha's face, still glued to the window. *And now she can watch the same pomp and circumstance, which I did as a child, that's gone on for generations.*

"How are my two favorite girls? Did you save me any Scotch eggs?"

"Daddy! Daddy!" Lindley's voice was the first thing that had distracted Samantha all morning.

"Did you see them putting up the trees? Did you see how they have an assembly line to do this? Did you...,"

Jenn's questions were halted by her husband holding up his camera and patting it. "I'm not a photographer for nothing," he jokingly chided.

"Daddy! Daddy!" Samantha screamed again. "Look!" She pointed out the front window.

"I see! I see!" Lindley responded, mocking her high-pitched voice. "May I have a bite?"

"Uh-huh," the child answered without looking at him. Her eyes were again glued to the action outside the window.

"I see it was a successful trip," he observed.

"Sure was," Jenn nodded. "Look. See how they

drape those heavy electrical cords that hold all the wires from tree to tree?" She was pointing to the elm trees that lined the Green. The electrical cords were being bundled, taped together and strung through the high limbs of the trees to keep people from tripping over them. Like every other element of this process, it had been tuned to a fine art.

Lindley's eyes focused on the long line of Christmas trees. "Where do they get all those trees? They all look exactly alike."

"There's a place in Warren, 'Angevine Tree Farm,' Dad said, that donated all the trees for the Green. The men went and cut them down last week. They also get trees from Crystal Springs Tree Farm in Leighton, Pennsylvania, to sell at the church for a fundraiser. They've been selling those trees for years." Jenn gave a laugh. "Where do you think I get our tree every year?"

"I don't know. I never thought much about it. I guess I figured it was your job to find the tree and get it home, and my job to decorate it and take it down after Christmas."

"Those men at the church sell about six hundred trees every year. That has been the big fundraiser at the church for years."

"I'm terribly sorry to interrupt," stated the restaurant's host, "but how are they getting those trees to stand up? You know, we have really high winds sometimes in the winter. Why, I've seen them sometimes upwards of sixty miles an hour." He was still full of questions.

"Here," offered Jenn. "Why don't you go out there with me and I'll give you a demonstration?"

"How do you know so much about this?" he inquired.

"Because I've only seen it since I was about Samantha's age," she smiled.

She walked straight to the middle of the Green where two men were in the process of standing one of the trees. "See this?" Jenn pointed to an iron pipe that was being driven into the ground by one of the men. "They drill a hole in the bottom of the tree's trunk and it goes onto this iron pipe. Then they take quarter-inch wire, which comes from the local agri-cultural store, and anchor the tree to these smaller stakes that go off to the sides. There's five stakes here. See?" Jenn stooped to the ground, with Samantha following her lead. "Three on the north side, two on the south side."

One of the men halted his rhythm of slinging the sledgehammer. "We've always done it this way ever since I can remember and it seems to work. Last year we had winds of sixty-six miles an hour, and only one tree was bent over at the end of the storm."

"It's similar to putting up the tents at the B-Water Fair each year," the restaurant host noted. "I help the volunteer firemen there each year."

"Exactly!" Jenn confirmed.

"Hey, can we try that?" Two boys, appearing to be ten or eleven years old, had come with their father to help with the trees.

"Sure!" agreed the man who had stopped to talk as he handed one of the boys his hammer.

The man turned his attention to the next generation of tree workers for the Green as Jenn went back to her explanation of the process.

"From what I understand, Angevine Tree Farm has donated the trees for three years. Before that, I think Skitch and Ruth Henderson donated them a couple of times or so. Last year, the first tree on the south end was covered all in yellow lights in support of our troops."

"I had to take a shot of that last Christmas," Lindley interjected. "I'll never forget how difficult it was to capture my emotions of seeing those lights against the background of a snowy Green and the sign on the bandstand that read, "Remember Our Troops," with the sign under it that read, "God Bless the USA." His face indicated that the experience still rang strongly through his heart and soul.

"I get that same feeling each year when I come

to put up the trees," said a man walking up behind them. "I'm not even a member at the Methodist Church any longer. We moved to another town a few years back, but I still come to help every year. I remember watching the faces and the eyes of all the children on the first year that I helped with the trees." He paused. "Just like your daughter there. That's what hooked me and I've been here every year since."

A woman walked up behind the man. She had an armful of lights. "I've wanted to help with the lighting of the Green every year, but I had to work at the library and watch it happen from the windows. This year I was off, and I've been waiting for days for this opportunity." She glanced at Samantha. "Do you like the trees?"

Samantha grabbed her mother's hand. "Uh-huh." Her eyes were on her grandfather as he moved from tree to tree, making sure that everything was working as planned.

Vroom... Vroom... Vroom...

The sound of a familiar engine caught Jenn's attention before the shiny black 1970 Monte Carlo turned the corner from Route 7 onto the Green's Main Street.

"Triple black, all restored," the newspaper had reported about it. "A built 350 engine with over 400 horsepower, a racing cam, aluminum heads, a high manifold and 4 block headers with a 3" exhaust. The engine has roller rockers." Jenn knew the description verbatim.

She looked down at the engagement ring that once belonged to her grandmother, and that now sat perched, again, on the ring finger of her left hand. *Thanks to that engine.* The article about the Monte Carlo sounded like something from a sports section, but it had actually been the account of how Rich Tomascak had been a town hero in the capture of her stolen ring.

Jenn watched now as Rich parked in one of the Green's parallel spots and emerged from the car. *He looks exactly like Robert Mitchum in "Thunder Road." All he needs is a hot rod from the fifties.*

Rich Tomascak did look exactly like Robert Mitchum, so much so that given the fact of his more modern "hot rod," he could have very easily starred in a remake of that 1950's movie. His black hair had the same wave, he wore his shirts with the short sleeves rolled up and the top buttons undone.

Yes, he could have very easily stepped out of the James Dean era. Jenn watched as the quiet, unassuming man went straight for the ladders and began to climb them, stringing the heavily taped cables of wires from tree to tree. *The same job he's had since I was a child.*

She then noticed another man, Ralph Williams, a young man close to her age, take his place in holding the ladder for Rich. *Working together, side by side.* The sight was akin to the day Jenn's ring was recovered. It was the two of them who were credited with stopping the thief and capturing the ring.

The ring sat glistening on Jenn's finger as if it were proud to have played such a role in this memory, and more so, that it was glad to be back on the finger of its rightful owner. It became the object of the newspaper's cover story when it was stolen from a New York City jewelry store where she had taken it to get it cleaned. Since her grandfather had purchased the ring for her grandmother in the city, and that is where Lindley had the matching band made, that is where she'd wanted to have the routine cleanings done. A tradition, of sorts.

One day after she'd dropped off the ring and was doing some shopping in the city, some guy managed to get in the back door of the jewelry shop and take a number of pieces that had been left there for repair. Her grandmother's heirloom ring happened to be one of those pieces.

Thinking back on her horror at learning of the ring's disappearance, Jenn ran her finger across the beautiful antique setting of the ring. The ring she had now vowed would never leave her sight again, no matter what kind of work was being done on it. She looked back at the two men, still working side-by-side.

The sight of them took her back to a Saturday from the past August and the B-Water Fair. A day, shortly after the ring's theft, when she and Lindley had decided it would be a fun family event to take Samantha to the fair for the first time. The day that was to be the beginning of a family tradition for many years to come. The day that Kevin O'Neill, the police officer she'd seen on the Green, served Samantha her bowl of homemade ice cream.

Unbeknown to Jenn, Kevin was in the tent serving homemade ice cream as a cover-up in conjunction with the Bridgewater Police Department, who had gotten a tip about a couple of suspicious guys in the area. It seemed the two men were trying to pawn off merchandise suspected as stolen.

The men had last been seen in the vicinity of the fairgrounds, and with all the crowd gathered there, most of them with their attention on all the rides, food and exhibits, the policemen figured it would be a logical place for the men to get away from public attention.

Since Kevin worked the fair each year to help the local fire stations, he was chosen to do his annual job of serving ice cream. No one would suspect it out of the ordinary if they saw him in the tent with an apron and ice cream scooper. Even Mary Clancy, the woman who worked beside him each year in the tent, had no clue that anything was going on under her tent besides the scooping of ice cream into plastic bowls.

Jenn and Lindley had finished their ice cream and were watching Samantha go around in one of the little airplanes, next to the ice cream tent, when they saw Kevin take off running behind the logger's display arena. He was talking into a two-way radio as he headed for the path between the tractor exhibit and the sheep-shearing tent. There happened to be an exhibition in progress on how border collies worked with the sheep when Kevin spotted two men who matched the description he'd been given.

When the men saw Kevin running toward them, they took off toward the woods at the back of the fairgrounds. The police officer paused only long enough to ask the dog trainer if the dogs could corner people as well as sheep. Within an instant the dogs were in hot pursuit of the men, who had circled around the grounds and were on their way to the parking lot farthest from the activity. They obviously had a car parked there and were close to escape.

Thankfully, Ralph - who had overheard the policeman's radio conversation, and who'd attended the same church as Jenn since childhood - had a deep appreciation for tractors and had acquired his own collection of restored ones. Thankfully, also, the B-Water Fair still carried on its tradition of having an array of antique farm equipment sitting on the hill for spectators to view.

Ralph, who'd been watching the border collie exhibition, jumped on one of the tractors and took off toward the brush behind the field, with people moving to one side or another to make a way for him.

"Where are you going?" yelled Rich, who was also watching the collie exhibit.

"To catch a thief!" came a confident reply.

"On that old thing?"

But the *putt-putt-putt* of the tractor's engine was all Rich heard as Ralph cleared his own path in a hot pursuit. He ran for his Monte Carlo, which was parked in the lot across the road from the front entrance of the fairgrounds. Spinning tires as he left the parking lot, he was behind the car with the two men in short order. But it was Ralph, anticipating the men's actions, who pulled the tractor out from the field beside the fairgrounds and onto the road in front of the escaping men. The driver of the getaway car gave a sharp right turn to avoid hitting the tractor's front scraper, causing his speeding vehicle to career into a tree.

Rich jumped out of the Monte Carlo. "Looks like he did a bit of plowing of his own," he noted, seeing the path of grass and sod that lay upturned by the crashing vehicle.

Ralph hopped off the tractor. "We'd better call the cops. Trees have a way of not giving. Hope they're not hurt."

"No need to call the cops," spoke a male voice from behind them.

Rich and Ralph turned just in time to see a policeman getting off a bicycle and a black-and-white border collie running along behind him. The dog crouched down, creeping slowly up on the car, a soft growl in its voice.

Lindley, always with a camera, had followed Kevin on foot and was able to get shots of the entire episode. He had no idea who the men were, nor why they were being chased, but he made sure they'd be recognized from their photographs.

"Pretty good teamwork," called Kevin, as he moved up beside the wrecked car.

"Yeah! Just like in the movies." Rich held a hand out to Ralph. "I owe you an apology. I didn't think you could catch them on that old piece of metal. Guess you fooled me."

"It's just they were so busy watching you and that mean machine in the rearview mirror that they didn't see me until it was too late. You created the perfect diversion."

Spectators who had gathered weren't sure if this was a scene using one of the local Hollywood stars who lived in Bridgewater, or a "real" unexpected event. They were jabbering back and forth and trying to decide whether this had been planned or whether they had witnessed a crime being solved. The arrival of two squad cars, followed by a news van, answered that question for them.

"What would you have done had they hit you?" Kevin asked, turning to Ralph. "That could have been a very dangerous situation for you."

"I figured this old Allis-Chalmers had more to it than their little tin rattle trap," Ralph smiled. "They don't make them like this baby anymore." He patted the side of the tractor and then climbed back on it. "I'd better get this thing back before its owner sees it missing."

"You mean this tractor isn't yours?" Kevin's voice rang with disbelief.

"No, but I'd always wanted to drive one. Guess I've had my chance now. Are you going to write me up, Officer?"

Kevin didn't get time to answer.

"Lindley!" Jenn's voice was so shrill that she could hardly be heard. "Lindley!" she huffed. "Look!"

With Samantha in her arms, she was running as hard as she could toward the crowd gathered around the car and the two men.

She held out her left hand and showed him her ring, her grandmother's heirloom ring. "They just tried to sell Grandmother's ring to a couple back there. They told the woman to try it on, and they didn't have time to get it back before they took off running. I saw the ring in the woman's hand and told her what had happened. Luckily, Rich's wife, Ruth Ann, recognized the ring and verified my story."

A couple of other police cars pulled up to the accident. Kevin walked toward them. "It appears we may have caught a jewel thief, Captain."

Within minutes, the men were arrested and their trunk was found to have many of the other items that had been stolen with Jenn's ring, along with some other goods that had been picked up along the way.

"Looks like these boys got more than cotton candy at the fair. They're going to have a souvenir they can remember for a long time," one of the police officers told Kevin. "A nice stay behind bars."

Now, in the cold November air that was quite different from that hot August afternoon, Jenn thought back through that entire scenario. It wasn't the disappearance, or even the capture, of the ring that stood out in her mind. It was Pop's reaction to the whole thing. She had been terrified about telling him of its theft, fearing his tremendous pain rather than a bout of anger.

Yet he never once blinked an eye. His only words were, "That ring is protected by sixty-three years of a blessed marriage. It was my Martha's ring. It will come home."

At the time, Jenn didn't understand how he could appear so unconcerned. When she rushed to show Pop it had been reclaimed, after all the paperwork had been filed and the insurance company and jewelry store had been notified, he simply nodded.

He never said, "I told you so." He merely said, "That ring is blessed by sixty-three years of love." There had never been a doubt in his mind that the ring would be found.

The local media all ran stories of the miraculous recovery. They described Rich's car as if it had gone on a wild chase after the thieves, although it was only around a curve and up a short stretch of road. But it had been enough for him to hit 75 mph in a few seconds and catch the attention of every muscle car fan at the fair.

Or that read the paper, she surmised as she continued to ponder on that afternoon. She, too, had read the article. Enough times that the description of the triple black '70 Monte Carlo was forever etched on her mind.

Another wonderful thing about living in this small hometown community, she reflected as she watched the two rescuers of her heirloom now work together with a team of other men. *People are ready to lend a hand, to help others, to be a part of things, while at the same time, they stick to their own business.*

She looked down the row of Christmas trees, most of which were all decorated and ready to be an integral part of the holiday season's history. Jenn had been so wrapped up in her thoughts of the ring that she hadn't noticed her father approaching until now.

"Morfar, morfar!" Samantha took off toward her grandfather, her arms extended into the air, ready to be swooped off her feet by the familiar figure.

"Ready for a donut?" Dave looked at Jenn and Lindley. "It's time for the men to take a break and get their second wind. Some coffee is going to taste and feel good about now."

"Donut," repeated Samantha. "Want donut."

Lindley walked alongside Dave to retrieve and help carry the coffee and donuts for the workers. "That is quite an assembly line you have going there," the son-in-law stated. "I don't know that I've ever seen workers that in tune with each other."

Dave nodded proudly. "They do understand

the art of working together. That's a big problem with the country today. People don't know how to work, and they don't *want* to know how. Very few people adhere to Pop's theory of work."

"You mean the one about eight hours of work for eight hours of pay?" Lindley had obviously, at some point in time, heard the elder gent make his infamous statement on the work ethic.

"That would be it. There's no doubt in my mind that he never wasted a minute when he was on the time clock. My father worked hard and made an honest day's living, but he knew how to rest and relax. I think that's why Pop's still in such good health today. He took long walks, *relaxing* walks, every single Sunday. Not like the power walks people go on these days, but a walk that was slow and tranquil. A walk that allowed him to see and hear everything around him, and to actually become a part of it. I'm sure those walks aroused every one of his senses as he smelled the warm earth or the freshly mown grass, the roses or the nearby horse stables. He saw the budding trees and bulbs blossom into fruit and flowers. He heard children at play in their yards instead of in front of their computers. He tasted the honeysuckle and the berries. He felt the nip in the air and the hot summer's heat."

Dave stopped right in front of the Bank Street

Coffee House and began to hum *Blott en dag.* "And he sang and thanked God for all of it. The beautiful and the despicable, the fragrant and the putrid, the roar and the melody, the hot and the cold, the delicious and the bitter." He opened the door of the coffee house. "He sang thanks for all of it."

"Dad's right," Jenn confirmed, turning to Lindley. "I don't ever recall Grandpa ever uttering a cross word or saying something unkind about another individual. He felt that everyone and everything were God's creatures and he respected that." She looked at the open newspaper laying on the table with the morning's headlines all telling of the troubles of the world.

Lindley could read her thoughts. "Too bad there are not more people like him now."

Jenn only nodded. She reached out and took Samantha from her father while he purchased the coffee. "All things bright and beautiful," she began to sing to her daughter, remembering the words of a children's hymn she had learned when she was Samantha's age.

As they headed back to the Green to bear cups of warmth and cheer to the workers, Jenn looked at Lindley. "Too bad there aren't as many beautiful things today as there were in Pop's years as a young father."

She stopped, dead in her tracks, as Samantha began to kick furiously and point. All of the lights on the row of Christmas trees came on as one of the men pulled the switch to check them. A joint gasp could be heard from across the Green.

"Perhaps there are," Lindlay observed as he extended an arm of love, comfort and joy around his wife and daughter.

CHAPTER 15

It was a well-known fact among the citizens of New Milford that Christmas was, by far, the most beautiful and peaceful season on the Green. This year was no different. The snow made it difficult for some to travel, but by the same token, it also made a most elegant backdrop for the Blue Spruce, Douglas and Frazer fir trees covered with the old-fashioned large light bulbs.

They were the same bulbs that had been used for generations, but they'd never lost their brilliance against the darkness of the horseshoe-shaped village. Even with the modern day's decorations of the white miniature, twinkling varieties, it was decreed that the lights on the Green were a tradition; they were of various colors and they did not twinkle. Plus there was a rare beauty about them, and "the way it had always been."

That's pretty much the way it is with Pop in the winter of his life! Jenn reflected. *In a time when the work ethic has changed drastically from the Old World beliefs, and people try to see how much they can cram into one day, he still follows his philosophy of "one day at a time."*

The reflective granddaughter unknowingly took a deep breath, exactly as Pop did when he took things in. With her exhalation came a smile, also a trait of her grandfather's. *He is such a gift of rare beauty. Yes,* she thought, *that's a perfect way to look at it. He's even surpassed the beauty of his life into that "rare beauty" stage.*

Jenn didn't tarry on the benches this day. She made a swift dash from her car to the warmth of The Grand Patisserie and a bowl of soup. *The biggest difference in the Green,* she snickered, once inside, *is that the benches are empty in the wintertime. You can sit wherever you like because everyone else simply drives through, takes a good look at the trees and then moves on.* It wasn't that they were in a bigger hurry, or that they rushed through the motion. The cool "nip," to put it mildly, simply kept people moving at a faster clip than usual.

She had taken the afternoon off to finish her shopping. It was amazing how successful she'd been in finding just the right gift for everyone on her list, given all the time she'd spent parked on a bench on the Green, rather than shopping, back in the fall. She was aware that many would have reflected upon that week and said, "*should* have spent shopping." But in looking over all of life's lessons she learned on that bench underneath those trees, she knew that week had been spent *exactly* where it "*should* have been spent." She had been given a choice, and fortunately, *and blessedly*, she had made the right one.

Now she only had a few things left to get, one of which was her own present to be from Samantha. She would pick it out, then take her daughter shopping after daycare and let Samantha carry the gift and pay for it. Then Lindley would help Samantha wrap it and put it under the tree.

Probably the same as thousands of other mothers, she chuckled inside. *My gift to myself is the treat of a quiet lunch.*

Jenn inhaled the aroma of the freshly baked bread and felt the steam of the chowder rise against her face. She watched as a couple of youngsters on the Green braved the cold and threw snowballs at each other. *I remember doing that. Seems like I didn't mind the cold a bit.* She was willing to bet these two guys didn't notice it, either.

I'll bet Samantha doesn't notice it, either. I'll have to bring her by here this weekend. The evenings are too cool…for me, at least.

"Hello, hello, Mrs. McCaughan!" called a firm, yet bright voice.

Jenn looked up. She'd been so busy enjoying the snow scene that she had failed to notice Axel Karlsson enter the small café.

"Mr. Karlsson, how nice to see you."

She had admired this man for as long as she'd known him. Through a college scholarship fund he'd started years earlier, he continued his practice as an avid supporter and encourager of the youth of New Milford's United Methodist Church. Not only that, Mr. Karlsson was a dear friend of Pop's. She had heard them swap many Swedish stories over the years.

"Mind if I join you?" he asked.

"No, please do," offered Jenn. "I'd feel slighted if you sat anywhere else."

She watched as this family friend placed his order. Ever since she'd known him, he had possessed a distinctive stride. Not a boastful carriage, but merely one of pride in his ancestry and his native town. If anyone knew anything about New Milford, *along with Libby Porter!*, it was Mr. Karlsson.

No wonder he was the President of his senior class

in high school. His carriage portrays the looks and the charisma of a natural-born leader.

"A beautiful New Milford winter day, isn't it?" he asked as he placed his tray of lentil soup and hot buttered bread on the table and sat in the chair opposite her.

"Yes… yes, it is," she smiled. Jenn had not thought of the day as beautiful. It was a typical cold, snowy New England winter's day. But at the same time, it was a textbook example of a winter in the countryside of western Connecticut. She glanced out the front window at the two boys who had been joined by a cluster of others. "It is indeed a beautiful winter day."

They joined hands and said the table blessing that they'd both learned as children. "God gud, valsigna maten, i Jesu namn, Amen."

Jenn sensed an overwhelming comfort as she conceived that this Swedish blessing, "Merciful God, Bless this food in Jesus' name, Amen," had come all the way around the world with her grandfather and Axel's father.

"This is a great table," stated Mr. Karlsson. "We can sit here and admire the Town Hall. I love that building."

Jenn knew this man well enough to know that tone of voice. It meant she was in for a tidbit of trivia.

"Did you know that building was the home of Roger Sherman?" he asked. "Right there. Sherman was the only person to sign the four documents that began our country. The Declaration of Independence, the Articles of the Confederation, the Bill of Rights and the Constitution. Yes," he nodded, "the one and only."

"My favorite house in town is the yellow one next to the Masonic Lodge that once served as the Episcopal Church." Jenn wanted to make sure Mr. Karlsson recalled leaving her with that bit of history the last time they'd met on the Green.

"Ah, that yellow house. Do you know that it used to sit on the corner next to Elizabeth's?"

Jenn shook her head, anxious to hear the story of the house she loved.

"They moved it right up the Green. Clem Noble moved it, he did. I remember that thing. I remember it going right up the center of the road there. It was on big rollers with pneumatic tires. Strangest thing I ever saw going up the Green."

Jenn laughed. She remembered how much the youth loved the many stories Mr. Karlsson would tell, before and after the UMYF meetings, when he and his wife, before her passing, were counselers.

"What about the stores? Was there any place to shop besides the Village Hardware?"

"There surely was! We'd go into Warner and Disbrow's. They had sawdust on the floor because it was a butcher shop. There was this big barrel of dill pickles right in the front corner. I loved to go in there and take the pair of tongs, reach in the barrel and get out a pickle.

"And there was Golden's. My mother always shopped at Golden's. Do you know that when the Depression hit, he never cancelled her credit? She would go in and pay as she could, and Mr. Golden allowed her to dress us kids and get whatever she needed. Because of his kindness and graciousness, she was one faithful customer. Shopped there her whole life."

Jenn stared into the face and eyes of the man seated across from her. There was a rosy tone about his round cheeks, and big blue eyes that still sparkled with the enthusiasm of a young boy.

Looking at that face, she remembered a tale from one of her elementary classmates, who lived across the street from Mr. and Mrs. Karlsson. The boy would come to first grade nearly every day with bragging rights about Mr. Karlsson - "Mr. K," the boy called him - and his orange Jeep.

"Mr. K" would take the young boy, who was like a son to him, riding in the Jeep. The horn was hidden on the steering wheel, so Mr. K would blow it, with his knee, without the child's knowledge. For three years, Jenn's classmate was sure the orange Jeep possessed magical powers.

Alone with this kindly gentleman, she could see that his sense of charm was mixed with a great humor. *And a generous helping of sensitivity,* she knew from experience, having been in his youth group.

"How's Pop? I miss seeing him at church these days."

There's that question, speaking of magical! Jenn had been waiting for the subject of the patriarch of the Kullgren clan to surface.

"He's doing fine. You know him, always fine. I think if it were left up to him, he'd still be right there every Sunday on that same pew where he's sat for years." *Like Libby's magical Number 7 Pew!* "But we all coddle him a bit. We insist that he stay inside where it's warm during these cold months. Too many germs, and that sort of thing, you know."

"Yes, I do know. I try to be careful myself this time of year. I think when one reaches this season of life, they begin to think of those precautions more."

Season of life? How interesting to hear him speak of it that way. Seems like "seasons of life" is all I've thought of lately.

"The thing I miss most about seeing Pop every Sunday," Mr. Karlsson continued, "is the way he'd walk down the center aisle, very dignified, like in a parade or a procession. He'd always stop for a brief moment when he'd pass the pew where my brother and I sit, two pews back from where he sat, and say, 'Hur mar du?' which meant, 'How are you, Axel?'

"I'd try to respond with something clever like, 'Som fin sneu,' which meant, 'As fine as snuff.' He'd grin a little bit and then walk on down the aisle to his pew." Mr. Karlsson smiled. "We've shared that little routine every single Sunday since I've known him. I looked forward to our ritual every week."

"I'm sure it meant just as much to Grandpa," Jenn assured, causing Mr. Karlsson to grin a little bit.

"Yes," he paused.

Jenn could tell from the expression on Mr. Karlsson's face that, in his mind, he was seated on his usual pew in the sanctuary with Pop standing beside the pew and leaning on his cane, held in front of him with both hands propped on the top of it.

"I can see him now. Those huge hands resting on that cane as he stood there and shared that friendly bit of conversation with me. That's the one thing that stands out in my mind the most about Pop. The size of his hands. I don't believe I've ever seen hands that large on anyone. Such strong hands. No wonder God chose him for a carpenter."

"Or maybe the order was, God chose him for a

carpenter, therefore He blessed Grandpa with big hands."

"I'm sure you're right about that. They say that some people have some awfully big shoes to fill. With Pop, it's that he has some mighty big hands to fill."

Jenn nodded.

"When I'd ask how he was, Pop's answer was, 'Fin, thah!' No question. Simply, 'Fin thah!' And then he'd say, 'I take it one day at a time,' because I didn't know those words in Swedish. Pop never seemed to lose one bit of his ability to speak or read Swedish."

"That's exactly what everyone said to us on our visit to Sweden. They were impressed by his memory of the language. I think it's because he learned to sing the language as soon as he learned to speak it."

Neither of them spoke for a few minutes as they enjoyed the succulent grain flavors, blended in the bread, and the freshness of the soup.

"Is Pop still singing?" Axel finally asked.

"Every day," Jenn answered with a smile. "He sits in his recliner and listens to his CDs, singing along with each one of them."

"In Swedish, I'll bet."

"Yes." Jenn's voice had a cheerful lilt. "He still remembers the words to every single one of those hymns, all in Swedish, even though he's been in

America for years. They say you remember the songs you learned as a child much more readily than other things, but him and his music… it's the most amazing thing I've ever seen."

"You know, that man *is* the most amazing man I've ever seen in my life," Mr. Karlsson reminisced. "I've known other people who have lived to see the century mark. Or a couple, I should say. I well recall, as a boy, watching the Veteran's Day Parade every year and seeing Mr. Charles A. Way riding down the street, sitting in a convertible and waving to all the crowd. He would be all wrapped up against the cool of the air, blankets and throws covering his woolen topcoat and suit, with his hand motioning in a wave to the people.

"I'll never forget that wave. There would be that hand, that paper-thin hand, up in the air, slowly waving back and forth. He was the town hero, for he had fought in the Civil War. Everyone knew Mr. Charles A. Way. And that's exactly what he was called. Charles A. Way. I never did know what the 'A' stood for. I'm not sure anyone else did, either, but you never heard his name spoken without it. Mr. Charles A. Way," he repeated again, this time with a nod and an imitation of the man's wave of his hand.

"But Pop is not like him. Your grandfather is nearly one-hundred-and-two years old, and he still has that same tall stature. Not a slouch about him at all. No sirree," Mr. Karlsson smiled.

That's what it was about Pop that Jenn had not been able to put her finger on. *His stature.* She had never known anyone of that age before, but she had known people less than his age. Some of them were shriveled up, or unable to get around. And here was her grandfather, still getting up, getting dressed, making his bed and fixing his own breakfast.

"You're right about Grandpa," Jenn noted. "It is amazing. What I find interestingly comical is how he always has to have something different each morning for breakfast. He eats better than I do," she laughed, "and I prepare meals and menus at the club for a living."

Mr. Karlsson joined her laughter. "You're right. I've sat beside Pop at church dinners. I sat beside him at the spaghetti supper just a couple of months ago and he could still put away the food."

"Yes, he can. He asks for seconds at many meals, or at least for dessert. We'll be seated around the table, eating dinner, and he'll pipe up before any of the rest of us finish and ask, 'Is there any dessert?' I love it!"

"The most amazing thing I ever saw," Mr. Karlsson reiterated. He looked out the front window and saw the group of boys that had congregated on the snowy lawn. "Just like when I was a boy."

"You played out there in the snow, too?" Jenn asked, an element of surprise in her voice. She quickly apologized. "I'm sorry, I didn't mean that like it sounded. It's that I'd just been thinking about how I played out there as a child."

"No need to apologize. Every kid in New Milford must have played out there as a child."

Jenn could hear another story coming from Mr. Karlsson. It was a trait of the Swedes she had learned to recognize from her grandfather. There was a lilt that began with their speech that signaled the listener that they were getting in gear to roll off a story.

"Boy, oh boy, how well I remember playing in the snow when I was growing up. When I was little, the policemen would close off the sidewalks at dark and kids would come out of the woodwork, I'll tell you. They'd be lined up all the way back around Elm Street with their sleds and toboggans, ready for a ride to remember. The adults and younger children would line the streets, screaming and yelling, 'Here comes another one!' a warning for the sledder in front to keep moving.

"Ha! There was no chance of stopping. If you got a good running start, you could go all the way down the hill to the end of the Green, make a turn and slide downhill all the way to the bridge down

Route 7."

Jenn stared at him in amazement. "You mean the bridge all the way down at the McDonald's."

"I sure do! There was not much out that way then and once we got going, there wasn't much way to stop… unless you crashed, of course. And no one wanted to do that. He'd have been the low man on the totem pole, for sure."

"Do you have any idea how far that was? It must have been over a mile."

"More like two," Mr. Karlsson boasted. "Ah, what wonderful memories."

"I remember you for years helping put up the Christmas trees. I guess little boys never outgrow playing on the Green in the snow, do they?"

"Absolutely not!" He took another bite of his soup. "Umm. This is really tasty. Whoever's in the kitchen is a good cook." He took another spoonful. "My mother was a good cook." Mr. Karlsson shook his head. "No, she was a wonderful cook. You know what I think was most amazing about her and her skill of cooking? Even when times were hard, she knew how to make the food so that there was plenty for everyone in the family."

Jenn loved the expression on his face. She could nearly grasp an image of Mr. Karlsson's mother, the vision from the past was so clear in his eyes.

"She cooked a lot of fish. Swedes use a lot of fish, you know."

"Yes, I do know," she nodded. "I've had my share of herring."

Jenn's vision of Mr. Karlsson's mother grew to include his wife, Faye, who'd also been a vital role model in the lives of the youth of the church. At one time, she was actively involved with the UMW and each year would plan a Smorgasbord for the church, complete with Swedish flags. Her cooking was so good that Jenn could practically taste the herring.

"My Aunt Eva could cook more dishes using herring in different ways," Mr. Karlsson continued. "We never had roast beef or hamburger. And my mother, I think she was just as good at finding new ways to serve it. She'd make this one dish that was like stew beef with herring. Pickled herring. Mother would make it in a huge crock every Christmas. It had the consistency of stew beef. She'd put a lot of cream in the fish. Then she'd put in potatoes. Small potatoes, always boiled.

"Sill and potatoes. That's what you call it." He gave a lick across his lips. "You know, I can still taste that, it was so good."

"She'd take me up to the town of Washington. The town was one-third Swedish. They even had two Swedish Methodist churches – one across the street from the other. There was a store there where my mother would go. It was run by a German man, but he kept lots of Swedish food, especially around the holidays. 'Boder's Market,' it was called.

"Mother would go up there and buy the whole herring, she would. I remember this one time he had dried cod hanging on a hook in the window. It had flies hanging on it. There it hung, just like a piece of cardboard. You could have hit someone upside the head with it, it was so stiff!

"My mother could take a piece of fish like that and freshen it. To preserve it, the market had salted it, so she had to freshen it in the water to get all the salt out. Then she would make a cream sauce. It was still salty a little bit, even in the cream sauce, but I loved it. 'Lutefisk.' That's what we called it. Creamed cod."

"I had lunch with Roberta Buddle not long ago. She was talking about her mother making a grilled cod for Good Friday. It was the soft kind, in the box, but she talked about how her mother had to soak it. She said she could remember Good Friday distinctly, for she could smell the cod all the way through the house. Her mother served it with mashed potatoes and green peas, and Roberta said that to this day, she still loves mashed potatoes and green peas."

"We always had that at Christmastime." Mr.

Karlsson took the last bite of his soup, wiped his mouth with the napkin, then folded it and placed it on the table. "Christmastime… the big time for Swedes. I looked so forward to Christmas Eve. That's when we gave out our presents.

"I had two aunts and an uncle who would come down from Brooklyn. They would send their food down ahead of time by Parcel Post so that Mother could prepare it, and then they came by train for Christmas Eve and Christmas Day. Also by Parcel Post came gifts. We were a Depression family, so it would have been a lean Christmas had it not been for those aunts and that uncle. As it was, Christmas was wonderful. Every year, it was wonderful.

"And the food on Christmas Eve! The whole table on Christmas Eve was Swedish food. Swedish brown beans, all kinds of cheeses, anchovies, potatoes and ham. For Christmas, the pickled herring would be more of an appetizer. Um! Talk about a smorgasbord!

"The table was beautiful. The three ladies, my mother and my two aunts, would be in the kitchen all day making that stuff. I'll never forget those nights. And my favorite thing was always the sill." Mr. Karlsson didn't stop, even for a short breath. That youthful zeal that Jenn noticed had kicked into gear.

"I can see my mother in the kitchen just like it

was yesterday. She would put the herring in with onions, vinegar, whole black pepper, water and bay leaves. It would sit like that for three to four days. Maybe even four to five days. But it would sit there all that time. It wasn't mealy or slippery. It had a body to it, and it had a tang to it.

"Father would come home at lunch and he'd go in the kitchen, take a saltine cracker, and then reach into the sill with a fork and eat it. Just like that. Then off he'd go again in his truck."

He grinned."I didn't think of it as fish. Never associated it with fish because it was firm. It would last for about a month, but it would begin to get a little bit softer during that time. It's life was about three weeks."

Jenn was totally enthralled by the story she'd anticipated. She chuckled at the thought of dead fish, soaked in potatoes and onions, having a life at all, much less three weeks. And the vision of the cod, complete with flies, was hysterical to her. Mr. Karlsson's way of telling this tale was typically Swede, and she loved it. Suddenly, her heritage slapped her upside the head the same as if it had been that whole cardboard-like cod in the window.

What also slapped Jenn upside the head was the conclusion that she was spending her shopping time by sitting here, in a cozy warm café – a perfect setting for a New England winter's day – listening to tales of Christmases past. And the beautiful part of the story was that this was the greatest Christmas gift she could ever receive. There was no way she could find such a meaningful gift in a store, especially a mall, and there was no way to wrap such a unique and wondrous gift.

Kind of like the "real" gift of Christmas. She smiled gently at the man seated opposite from her, a remarkable man in his own right. "Mr. Karlsson, do you remember anything else about Christmas?" Jenn had decided that there was no way she was leaving this place until she'd heard "the rest of the story."

"Boy, do I!" That question served as an open invitation for Axel Karlsson to share his wealth of knowledge and memories with a captive individual. "Mother would make pies, starting at Thanksgiving and bridging all the way until Christmas. Apple, pumpkin, mincemeat… my goodness, you've never seen the like of so many pies. And cookies. She made all kinds of cookies for Christmas."

Even though she had just finished a hearty helping of soup and bread, Jenn's mouth was watering at the idea of the Karlsson kitchen. She could imagine the beautifully set table, piled high with baked concoctions that were every child's dream. Then she envisioned Pop. *Baked concoctions that were every child's dream, no matter* how *old they were!*

"And, of course, we made glogg," Mr. Karlsson continued, picking up energy as he relayed the story.

"Ah, yes… glogg!" Jenn gave a huge smile. "I think one would be un-Swedish if they didn't make glogg at Christmas."

Mr. Karlsson gave a robust laugh, reminding Jenn of Santa Claus. She thought of this man, with his vibrant personality and love for children.

He'd be perfect. She continued to smile, tempted to share her sudden image of a red suit with him, but decided better of it. *Another time.*

"We made our glogg in the bottom part of a turkey roaster," Mr. Karlsson explained. "And I can remember the recipe just like it was yesterday when my father was in the kitchen making it. He prided himself every year by telling us that this particular recipe for glogg came down from none other than King Gustav. King Gustav, himself!"

Jenn nodded, most impressed, as she wondered whether this was the same recipe her family used.

"He'd use one pint of Grave's alcohol – 125 proof. You'd get it in the drug store."

Already Jenn was losing her mental taste of delectable cookies from a moment ago.

"One bottle of red wine, one bottle of water and whole cinnamon sticks. Then he'd wrap up a piece of gauze filled with cloves with the heads off, cardamom seeds – you'd have to get those at the drug store, too – and one cup of raisins. He'd place the gauze in the roaster with all the other ingredients and heat them over the stove.

"You always served glogg hot. My favorite part was when it was time to serve the glogg. He'd save five to six drops of Grave's alcohol, pour it over a sugar cube, throw it in the pot and light it. The sugar cube melted down in the pot and the whole thing glazed up blue.

"And to think we were serving the very same thing as King Gustav. Now that was quite something, I'll tell you."

Jenn had never watched the procedure of the making of glogg, but this certainly gave her a greater appreciation of its background. Even though she was not a fan of the Christmas beverage, it was a part of the tradition that was saved for the patriarch's home.

"I remember my first breakfast at my Uncle Uhle's house in Sweden. There was a bowl of hard-boiled eggs, one of potatoes, one of pickled herring and one of chicken. Uncle Uhle took a cube of sugar and put in it his mouth, like a nip of tobacco, and sipped his coffee through it. I'd never seen anyone drink coffee like that before."

"What about the presents?" Jenn asked. "Did

you get toys?"

"Toys? Oh, sure. Santa Claus would come. 'Juhl Tomter.' That's what the Swedish call him, 'Juhl Tomter.'"

Jenn now vaguely remembered hearing that term as a child, but she had completely forgotten it. She could already tell that she was going to have to introduce Samantha to the traditions of Sweden. *Juhl Tomter*, she repeated in her head several times. *I'll stop by the library tonight on the way home and find a book of international Christmas stories.*

"Santa Claus, Juhl Tomter, would come and give out one present to each child in the family.

"Santa Lucia Day starts the Christmas season for the Swedes. On that day, the oldest girl comes out in a long white dress and serves coffee and pastries. First to her parents' house, then to the neighboring houses and friends. She wears a crown with candles. There's a song about Santa Lucia Day that all the children learn in Swedish, then they all march in a long line and sing it."

Mr. Karlsson's jovial expression changed to a much more serious one. "But it is very different there, in Sweden. You've been there with Pop, haven't you?"

"Yes." She was still imagining the vision of a Swedish Santa Lucia Day in her head. "Yes, I did go there for Pop's 95th birthday. The whole family went."

"I learned an appreciation for my family, for my ancestors, when I went over there," explained Mr. Karlsson. "I've been twice, and both times it was an eye-opening experience. Sweden is such a desolate country, especially in the winter months, that they need a long time of celebration. The sun hardly shines at all, at least in the middle of the winter. While I was there, I never saw the sun. The day simply trailed off to graduating levels of darkness."

"I'd never thought of it that way," Jenn noted. "But come to think of it, I don't remember seeing the sun while I was there, either. I was so caught up in watching Pop reunited with his family and his home that I guess I didn't pay much attention to the sun and the daylight."

Mr. Karlsson looked down at his watch. "Speaking of graduating into darkness, look how late it is getting to be. I didn't mean to take up so much of your time, Jenn."

"It was an absolute delight. I'm thrilled that you happened in here today. By the way, Mr. Karlsson, what were you doing out on such a cold and snowy day? I'd think you'd have rather stayed in the warmth of your home on a day like this."

"Yesterday was my seventy-ninth birthday. I came into town just so I could say "hello" to the guys at the fire station – they're like my family, you know – and treat myself to lunch. I absolutely love the pastries here." The kindly gentleman looked directly at Jenn's rich brown eyes. "And young lady, your company here today has given me the greatest birthday present I can ever remember. I haven't shared these stories with anyone in years." He gave his recognizable sideways smile. "In fact, I'm not too sure that I've ever shared them with anyone."

Jenn returned the smile, one that was full of appreciation, understanding and a sharing of a same cultural background. "And you, my dear fellow, have given me the best Christmas present I've ever had by sharing your stories."

She grabbed his hand, signaling him to stand, and pulled him to the glass case, lined with beautiful and assorted pastries all the way down the length of the café. "What would you like for your birthday? It's from me... and Pop!" she exclaimed proudly.

"Why, Mrs. Jennifer Kullgren McCaughan, that's the best offer I've had all day!"

The pair of celebrants chose three pastries, which they cut in half and shared. After a toast by Jenn for Axel's health and wealth for many more years, the two spent the next few minutes in chit-chat, much different from the conversation of the rest of the afternoon.

"Mrs. McCaughan, thank you for a lovely time. This is a birthday I shall never forget."

"Why, thank you, Mr. Karlsson. And thank you for the fascinating stories. This is a Christmas I shall never forget."

"How's my Samantha? Did you have a good time today?"

The little girl nodded her head with animated excitement.

"Did you hear a story?"

Samantha's head continued to nod.

"How would you like to go visit with Gammel Farfar?"

Now the feet joined the child's head in the fury of excitement.

Jenn had made up her mind, on the way to the Education Center, that the perfect end to this day would be to ask Pop about the Christmases he'd spent in Sweden.

Before the mother and daughter had a chance to sing through the child's favorite songs, they were pulling into the Kullgren driveway.

Samantha didn't even wait to get her coat off before she was bouncing through the house on her way to see her great-grandfather. "Gammel Farfar! Gammel Farfar!" She only stopped briefly to hug her grandfather, her "Morfar."

Jenn, on the heels of her daughter, reached down to give Pop a kiss on the cheek. She was not sure who had the more excited expression of satisfaction on their face, him or Samantha.

It's hard to believe the ravage of the country from the media's perspective when you witness the love that radiates in this household.

She pulled a wooden chair beside Pop. "Do you remember any stories from the Christmases you were in Sweden, Grandpa?"

"Story, story," echoed Samantha as she headed toward the den and her basket of books. "Read a story."

Dave heard the earnest plea from both his daughter and granddaughter, causing him to follow the youngster to the den. He wondered how many other men could relate to the luxury of telling a story to his granddaughter, while his father was in the next room, also telling a story to *his* granddaughter. *Four generations of telling stories under one roof.*

A sense of sanctity rushed through his veins as if this moment, this opportunity, were a part of his very existence. *It is*, he concluded as he opened a book to the first page. From the other room he heard an elderly man and a young woman deep in conversation. It was a memory that he hoped he would one day treasure as his own.

As Jenn backed out of the driveway and saw the silhouette of Pop's head in the front window, she reflected on her afternoon conversation with Axel Karlsson. A blissful chuckle of joyous tidings accompanied the decision that she would afford herself the privilege of having *two* wrapped presents under the Christmas tree this year. *A card noting a gift in honor of Mr. Karlsson, to the Youth Scholarship Fund, which he and his wife began at New Milford United Methodist Church, and a card noting a gift in honor of Harry Nils "Pop" Kullgren at the VNA.* A large smile spread across her face as she turned left onto Route 7.

Christmas shopping completed!

CHAPTER 16

The following October

*A*nother *autumn? Already? Seems like just yesterday that I was sitting on this same bench, trying to figure out what to do with my one free day.*

This fall day, Jenn came prepared. She had a new novel ready to be devoured, page by page. The day was incredibly reminiscent of the one from the previous fall, when she had come to the Green to have a day all to herself. She gave a casual chuckle as she compared the two days.

A year ago at this time, Pop was counting down the days until his next birthday, much like a child would have done, for his birthday brought about the granting of his life's last wish. Every day following that birthday was an even greater blessing, for it was another day that Pop could sit in his recliner and listen to himself sing on his debut CD, *This Is My Song*.

Another day that he could feel his heart stirred by the youthful moments he had shared with his family in his beloved Sweden. Another day that he could feel his soul moved by the beloved hymns that he had been taught by his musical parents and the Arvika congregation of the Swedish Methodist Church of his childhood. Another day that he could look at the albums, full of pictures of his beloved Martha, and the numerous cherished letters received from family members on previous birthdays. Another day that he could be proud to be an American. And, another day that he could get up and thank his beloved God for "one more day."

"One more day, one day at a time," Jenn could imagine in her grandfather's voice.

She turned to the first chapter of her novel and was momentarily blinded. The sun, basking down on her hand, caused her heirloom diamond to glisten so brightly that it reflected the sun's light back to the sky, flashing into her eyes on it's path.

A broad smile spread across her face as she briefly recalled the ring and the scenario behind its discovery. Her gaze rested back on her left hand as she stared past the gem's surface and into the far reaches of its facets.

I wonder when it was that I first noticed this ring. Was I a young child? Was I an adolescent?

Martha's ring had been a source of pride for Pop. "I got it in the city," he would tell the grand-children when one of them would ask about it. They all knew that "in the city" meant New York City.

Jenn recalled her grandmother's coy, girlish expression each time Pop would relay the story of how he wrote a letter to Martha's family in the "Old Country" to ask for her hand. "Because that was the proper way," Pop had replied once when questioned about the experience.

She also recalled the gratitude she'd heard from Pop and her parents each time they recounted the story of Lindley asking for her hand. That is when Pop informed him that she was to be given Martha's ring that contained sixty-three years of love.

Lastly, Jenn recalled that day, during her own wedding ceremony, when she looked down and re-alized that the band her husband placed on her hand was platinum to match the ring, rather than the less expensive metal they'd chosen.

Later, at the reception, when she questioned him about it, Lindley's only comment had been that he had to get the best to go with sixty-years of love. Both of them knew theirs was a marriage to pass any test of life, for it was ordained by the blessing of four centuries, not to mention their Father.

Meaningful experiences of Pop's life rolled in front of the reflective granddaughter's eyes like an orchestrated film show. Jenn closed her eyes and heard the accompanying sounds that represented each season of Pop's life. With a memory as vivid as if it had happened the day before, she envisioned Skitch Henderson in the bandstand, his hands the master of his Steinway, signed by five Steinway's. The one that he had played for over forty years on *The Tonight Show.*

The sounds coming from his fingers carried her from the Green to the Silo, the beautiful Sherman farm where Skitch and his wife, Ruth, had started a museum and a world-renowned cooking school. The farm where Skitch was famous for catering events for those of the community who volunteered their time for others. And the farm that, at the present, allowed Jenn a peacefully-drifting transition back to Arvika, Sweden.

Younger than Springtime was playing in the background as she envisioned Pop, milking the cow and chopping wood, on his small childhood farm. Then, with a hammer in his hand as he eagerly helped his father build something.

Summertime. Suddenly, the granddaughter was

back in America, stepping off a ship at New York's Harbor. There was a church in the background of the vision, with a bride in a beautiful white dress standing at the back door, preparing for the grandest walk of her life. A walk that would lead her into the most trying, most difficult, yet most blessed and beautiful adventure of her life. An adventure that would last the entire rest of her life.

An adventure that puts the "Survival" show to shame. That's real *survival – living with the same person for sixty-three years and still being in love.* The ring, blessed with all the years of that adventure, caught the sun in such a manner that it created a prism of light on Jenn's hand. *A rainbow. A rainbow of promise that no matter what comes my way, I can handle it.* She chuckled lightly. *One day at a time.*

Jenn noticed that the music in the background of her mind had changed. There were strains of *Ebb Tide* rolling her into the season of *Autumn Leaves.* Her mental voyage carried her to a quiet retirement community in Orange City, Florida, the scent of citrus hanging in the air from the limbs bent with fruit, ready for the picking.

Pop's thinning hair was lined with silver, but there was still plenty of life, just ready for the picking, even in the autumn of his life.

Jenn remembered the day her grandparents

came back to Connecticut to live at Butterbrook, a complex for retirees in New Milford. She, and her two brothers, were thrilled to again be near this couple that had meant so much to their lives.

"Except no more trips to Disney World!" Tom teased his grandfather.

Those days I loved to visit them on Friday, for that was the day of baked macaroni and cheese at the Windmill Diner. Jenn decided that come this Friday, Pop was having the daily special from the diner.

Winter Wonderland briskly jolted Jenn from Butterbrook and the Windmill Diner to the Green, decorated with all its trees, and snow blanketing the ground. *And the church parking lot with all the trees for sale.*

The church parking lot... the church...

The music stopped. Jenn's eyes opened and the daydream was gone. *So that's why my father was always involved in everything that went on at the church. That's why he and Pop were always at the church, Pop ready with his trusty hammer, ready to tackle any project that was needed.*

Pop had spent his entire working life with a hammer in his hand. He had worked for years at one of the large department stores in "the city," keeping it updated with the times, making it appealing to the customers who shopped there. Then he transferred to the United Nations Building where again, *with his hammer,* he took care of every repair and kept it in a magnificent state for all that took place within its walls. He helped to keep it the showcase it was for the world.

And with that same hammer, he gave his time to God's church. Repairing the walls and the facilities where souls would go to repair their lives.

Jenn realized that there was a trace of tears on her cheek. *That hammer that we presented to him in its own glass case for his 102ⁿᵈ birthday.*

Not until that moment had Jenn realized the magnitude of that hammer and all that it entailed. Pop's love for the church went far deeper than attending each Sunday and singing in the choir. It meant keeping God's house in perfect condition, out of a duty of respect to his Father – the same Father he'd had both in Sweden and in America – and out of a love for "the church." *The people.*

Those same people that Samantha depicts with her little wiggly fingers when she does the fingerplay, "Here's the church, here's the steeple…,"

She thought of how much time her own father had spent at the church. *And that love has been instilled in his sons.* Jenn's recollections stopped. *And a love that I must pass on to Samantha.*

Her visions were interrupted by passing voices.

"Isn't this the most beautiful cake you've ever seen?" Two women were walking down the sidewalk, admiring a birthday cake they'd picked up at the Grand Patisserie.

"And it's just as delicious," Jenn assured them. "Sabina made my grandfather's birthday cake."

The women walked on, thrilled that their cake was going to be the perfect compliment to a birthday party for their friend. "I can't wait to taste it," one called back over her shoulder to Jenn.

Can't wait to taste it? The comment catapulted Jenn's memory back to her grandfather and the life he had lived.

He didn't just "taste" life. He devoured it. He sampled all the finer things it had to offer. Not the finer things that money could buy, but the finer things of life. Love, patience, joy...

Jenn smiled. *The fruits of the Spirit.* Her smile grew to a small laugh. Her grandfather had never cared much for chocolate. He was always more into the cobblers, the fruit pies... *the fruits...of the Spirit.*

No wonder he has lived such a long and fulfilling life. He knew how to take it, to deal with it, to enjoy it... to savor it. She watched the two women walking away, still fascinated by Sabina's elaborate creation of pastry. *And no wonder we had her to bake Grandpa a cake topped with whipped cream, and fresh strawberries, kiwis and blueberries.*

The thought of the cake launched Jenn's memory forward to one final replay, a cherished day in the treasured annuls of her bank of times past. It was an unseasonably warm March 5th, only seven months earlier. So unseasonably warm that the event, originally scheduled to be held at New Milford United Methodist Church, was moved to the Green. The time was four minutes before the appointed hour of two in the afternoon. She sat holding a restless Samantha, whose energy and enthusiasm were mirrored by everyone else seated around them. It was a day unlike many of the people seated on the Green had ever seen. It was Pop's 102nd birthday.

The partying had begun the evening before with all of the out-of-town guests, which included numerous friends and family members, gathering at the Kullgren home for a dinner to commemorate the occasion. Then on the actual day of Pop's birthday, there had been a breakfast from eight until eleven in the church's Fellowship Hall. Immediately following the service had been a light lunch of sandwiches and salads for the family.

The day, in itself, marked a tremendous cause for celebration. For the last wish of Harry Nils Kullgren had mushroomed into a most memorable event. It would have been a most memorable event for anyone, but especially for someone of his age.

Pop's last wish, one that had been vocalized several times after his 100th birthday, had been to sing one more solo in church. His last wish had actually come true during the August of 2005, five months after his 101st birthday, at the hands of a stranger.

It was when a woman visited New Milford United Methodist Church as a guest speaker for their Women's Prayer Breakfast one Saturday morning. She visited the church because she had learned of Pop's desire to sing "one more solo" through one of her readers who knew this prince of a man. The woman, an author and musician, had been so touched by the fact that this man listened to her CDs and sang along, *in Swedish*, that she wanted to meet him. That's how the round-about way of the author also speaking at the church on the following morning, the Sabbath, came about.

"Or how God used each of the players to make this divine plan a reality," the author later said of the occasion.

The author, Catherine Guess, invited Pop to come to church that Sunday morning and sing a solo. He came, walked up to the piano bench, sat down beside her and sang *He Touched Me*. Though not a soul in attendance understood a word of the man's native Swedish, there was not a dry eye in the house –

including that of the author's. Every person seated in the congregation was, indeed, profoundly touched by the man's faith and keen sense of musicianship, both still very much evident in his singing of the hymn.

The solo became a part of the sermon when Catherine posed Pop as an example of using one's gifts and talents. She greeted the congregation, read the scripture and then gazed down at Pop with a sense of wonderment and grave humility. "Pop, if I had you at home with me in the Carolinas, I would record a CD of you and my son, also a second bass. He's about the same age as you were when you came to America, so he could be the 'Pop then' and you could be the 'Pop now.'"

Her comment was meant to serve as a light-hearted transition from Pop's stirring solo to the scripture and then to the sermon – which she vowed was unnecessary after the sermon he had provided through music. That one comment, however, turned into the most important statement delivered during Pop's life.

That is, besides Grandma's affirmative answer when he asked her to marry him, Jenn surmised. *Or should I say, when he asked her family?*

The comment was a large cause for much of the activity on the Green on Pop's 102nd birthday.

Jenn's focus returned to that Sunday afternoon, with a flock of people gathered on the Green, as she relived the occasion in her mind.

In her daydream, she rose from her chair, and handed Samantha to Lindley.

Then, like the author had been when she stepped up to the pulpit on that August Sunday morning, Jenn silently asked for help that her words to describe Pop would be powerful, yet sensitive. She prayed that her voice would also be clear and strong, uninfluenced by the emotion of the moment of this great and glorious celebration.

"C'mon, Grandpa, it's your big day!" she said as she took his arm and walked up the steps of the Green's bandstand with him. She led Pop to a chair that had been placed on the stage for him.

A hush came over the crowd as they saw this signal that the hour had come.

"Dear Grandpa," Jenn began, taking a note card from her pocket and fighting furiously not to succumb to the tears welling up inside her. She looked down at this man, on whose lap many children of the family had sat for generations, and felt the same calming assurance she had when she'd sat there as a little girl.

A sudden sparkle demanded her attention as she saw the sunlight reflecting off the diamond, *blessed with sixty-three years of joy before I ever got the chance to wear it.* Instantly, the strength of Martha, her dearly beloved grandmother, seemed as real to Jenn as if the woman were still alive and had placed her arm of support around the granddaughter's shoulder, an act she had performed many times in earlier years.

Jenn briefly looked into Pop's face with the admiration she remembered feeling the evening she'd gone through his photo album with Tom, David and Uncle George, the admiration she'd seen on the face of "the girlfriend" in Sweden, and an admiration she knew had only be surpassed by that on the face of Martha for sixty-three years. She glanced back at the glistening diamond and then over the crowd, whose eyes also lended support.

"Dear Pop, in honor of your 102nd birthday, I'd like to present you with this hammer." She paused and grinned. "It is actually the hammer of your father that was sent to us by your sister, Nancy, from Sweden. This hammer symbolizes the remarkable life you built during these 102 years. A life whose foundation was built by your own father in Arvika, Sweden. A life filled with love for your fellowman. And a life filled with dedication for your country." Jenn smiled at Pop. "Both of them."

David and Tom walked up the steps of the

bandstand and presented Pop with an American flag that had been sent to him by Governor Jodi Rell of Connecticut. Christopher and Jonathan, Uncle George's two sons, walked up behind them with a Swedish flag that had been sent by Pop's nephew who was an Admiral in the Swedish Navy.

Catherine Guess, who had flown in with her son for the celebration, followed them up the stairs and broke into a strain of *America, the Beautiful* on the piano, on loan for the day's celebration, as the crowd stood and sang. Pop stepped up to the microphone beside Jenn and also sang… in Swedish.

Following the third stanza of the hymn, which served as the beginning for a concert given in Pop's honor, the grandsons escorted Pop down the steps to a center-stage seat in the front row of chairs. A young man, Catherine's son Jamie, appeared from the audience and walked up the stairs, black Martin guitar in hand, and began to strum simple chords on the strings.

"Blott en dag," he sang in his second-bass voice, the notes reaching from the depths of his soul, just as they once had from Pop's soul, and Pop's Pop before him. After one stanza of Swedish, which only Pop understood, Jamie sang the English translation of the hymn's verses. "Day by day, and with each passing moment…,"

Pop sang every note and every word with him... in Swedish. When Jamie finished the song, his mother played a final rendition of the hymn in the parlor style in which it would have been done in Pop's youth. She completed the verse with a crescendo into a final refrain, which Jamie sang in Swedish as the coda. Each note swelled into a grand finale, painting the life Pop had lived through the notes, lilting and soaring, and pushing toward its ending, like Pop's life, being most magnificent with the final phrase, which translated said, "till I reach the golden land."

There was not a dry eye to be found on the Green as Jamie leaned his guitar against the rail of the bandstand and bowed to Pop in solemn awe and appreciation of a long life well lived. He then nodded to his mother, who gave the introduction into *How Great Thou Art*. One by one, the young bass sang through all of Pop's favorite songs until he had Dave and George to escort their father back up the steps of the bandstand.

"It's all yours, Pop," he said. "Take it away, Mom."

With no warning, Catherine rolled the broken arpeggios up and down the keyboard, notes which Pop clearly recognized. Jamie stepped down to the seats below, followed by Dave and George. Pop stepped up to the microphone and looked out over the Green, at all the trees that had stood there, tall and undaunted, for over a century – and some for two. They, too, had weathered the storms of life. Some were a little worse for the wear, but for the most part, they were still beautiful specimens of God's creation. Pop nodded toward them, as if to say, "We did it. We lived through it… we made it through… one day at a time… those were the days. I am blessed. Yep…,"

Then he began to sing, softly at first, but with his voice growing into a gentle crescendo, "Our Father, which art in heaven, hallowed be Thy name,"

It seemed the skies opened and a company of angels descended to join the final phrase, "For Thine is the Kingdom, and the Power, and the Glory forever," of *The Lord's Prayer*, the words which were first prayed by a carpenter many, many years before. By the final "Amen," there was no doubt in the mind of anyone at the Green that he or she had just witnessed a sight, and heard a voice, beyond imagination. They had come to give a gift, but rather, they had been the recipients of the greatest gift of all.

Thirty-one chimes of the church bells brought Jenn's thoughts back to the Green on a fall day with her new novel. She had been so wrapped up in the gift that her grandfather had given the world, and the gift that the world had given him, that she neglected to notice how late it was. Day was dying in the west as the sun exploded the sky with a rainbow of pastel colors that were swiftly graduating into neon glows before fading away into a gentle gray. There were only a few stragglers left, walking their strollers or dogs, along the long horseshoe corridor of a sidewalk.

This day had been much more than a day of a young mother reflecting on fond memories of her life and her family. Or even her newfound appreciation of the refuge and solitude found in the serene countryside that surrounded New Milford.

It had been a day of "living." Living by stopping to take a look at what life was all about. Living by basking on all the memories of things that really mattered in one's life. Living by *literally* stopping to smell the roses. Living by realizing that her life, like those of the leaves, would go through four beautiful and miraculously transforming seasons.

She looked up at the branches of the trees that sprawled out through the air like long fingers, spread wide to cover the grass, whose blades were now a softer greenish-gold than they had been back in the summer. Back in the summer when the Green was covered with people who had gathered to "stop and smell the roses," bearing picnic baskets and blankets or lawn chairs, the sound of music filtering through the air to transport them to a stress-free world for a few hours.

Due to the gusting breeze of the afternoon, there was only one leaf left on the tree above her head. One lone leaf bent toward the earth, seeing all those who had gone out in glory before it, to the ground below, and were now providing a soft cushion for the earth.

Jenn took in a long, deep breath, exhaling it very slowly as she stared at the leaf. Thrilling imaginary sounds from the bandstand began to trickle through her mind. Delicate treble sounds of skilled fingers rippling across the keys of a Steinway, and the beautifully enthralling bass voice of a man, over a century old, who had taught her how to not only live, but to truly know life and all of creation as a brother or a sister. Who had taught her soul to be still, to know, to listen.

The single remaining leaf suddenly fell loose from the tree, giving a grand performance, like that of a poised ballerina, as it flitted and danced through the air. Before it touched the ground, a last puff of wind whisked it up for a final swan song of soft rhythm and a graceful sway before it touched the ground. It lay there, beside the other leaves, its green turned to a shining glimmer of gold during the course of its four seasons of life.

Jenn looked at the bandstand, closed her eyes

again for a brief moment, and imagined Harry "Pop" Kullgren, *my Farfar*, his deep bass voice blending with the sounds of the rustling leaves, singing in his beloved Swedish. *"Blott en dag ett ogonblick I sander."* As she opened her eyes to walk away, she saw the leaves on the ground, all nestled together, where before they had hung limply on the branches and limbs of the trees. They, too, had known the opportunity of what it meant to *Be Still, My Soul.*

She turned toward the sidewalk and began to walk, down a trail she was sure had been walked by her grandfather in years past, looking up at the sky now colored by dusk. Stars were just beginning to peak through the grayish-blue. Soon the night sky would be bright with shimmering bursts of light, brothers and sisters of the earth, raining down upon creation, just as Pop had rained his shining light on everyone who had known him. *Or even known* of *him.*

Jenn cranked the van, backed out of the parking space and took one final look at where the last leaves of the season lay. *O Father God, may my light one day also shine like his.* As she turned right at the corner from the Green's Main Street onto Route 7, a path that had become familiar during the course of the past year, her eyes peered toward the heavens and her lips took the shape of a broad, reflective smile. She could hear the strains of a familiar old voice, following her through the air, where once the rustling leaves had joined it with sounds of *Be still, my soul…*

Blott en dag

Blott en dag ett ogonblick I sander,
Vilken trost, evad som kommer pa!
Allt ju vilar I min Faders hander,
Skulle jag, som barn, val angslas da?
Han som bar for mig en Faders hjarta
Giver ju at varje nyfodd dag
Dess beskarda del av frojd och smarta,
Moda, vila och behag.

Sjalv han ar mig alla dagar nara,
For var sarskild tid med sarskild nad.
Varje dags bekymmer vill han bara
Han som heter bade Kraft och Rad.
Morgondagens omsorg far jag spara,
Om an oviss syns min vandrings stig.
Som din dag, sa skall din kraft och vara,
Detta lofte gav han mig.

Hjalp mig da att vila tryggt och stilla
Blott vid dina loften, Herre kar,
Och ej trones dyra trost forspilla,
Som I ordet mig forwarad ar.
Hjalp mig, Herre, att vad helst mig hander,
Taga av din trogna fadershand
Blott en dag, ett ogonblick I sander,
Tills jag natt det goda land.

Text: Lina Sandell   Musik: Folkmelodi

Questions and Reflections

Working with Pop, especially the privilege of recording the CD, *This Is My Song*, with Pop, has taught me many lessons. Or, perhaps I should say, has reminded me of lessons that I already knew. He is a living example of the truths held in God's Word. It seemed quite in character for what had gone on with the rest of this book that as I finished writing it, I felt the urge to pick up my Bible, say a prayer and read a scripture in praise to God for the blessing of the completion of yet another book.

As I should have suspected, even that became a part of this book, for the passage I turned to was Matthew 6. Each word reminded me of the days I had spent with Pop, and the impressions he had left upon my life. Impressions that I knew would forever change my life. The reading of Matthew 6 was like watching Pop's life in action, and realizing that I was not the first person he had left his mark upon.

I knew from the moment I met Pop that it was love at first sight. He glowed with that special ambiance that only comes from a dear grandfather, and being that I had two wonderful grandfathers of my own, one of whom would have been the same age as

Pop were he still alive, there was a bond between us from the beginning.

I also knew that this book, meant as a tribute to Pop and a life well lived – truly the life of a "good and faithful servant," – had become one of life's greatest gifts to me. I have experienced many things in my life that I knew were blessings sent from God, things that I knew were for a particular reason or time, depending on my circumstances. Meeting Pop, writing this book and recording *This Is My Song* now head that list.

Be Still, My Soul and *This Is My Song* have already served as a gift to many people during their makings, and I'm sure, through their publication and production, will continue to do so for many others.

~ CR? ~

1)   Who in your life has been a messenger of God's truths?

(Keep in mind that this person can sometimes be a most unlikely character, possibly even someone who chooses not to follow God's Light, but someone who unknowingly has been chosen as a part of His plan to get your attention. Messengers - or more likely, the value of the truth or lesson they bring - can sometimes not be seen until "after the fact.")

What was God's message that was delivered through this person?

2)   Who in your life has been a living example of God's truths?

What lessons did this person teach you?

3)   In what areas of your life can you apply the principle of "one day at a time?"

Name an area where that phrase is evident.

Name an area in which you need to adhere that phrase.

4) What instance in your life has brought about a person (an old friend or a new acquaintance) whom you know God specifically placed in your path at a certain juncture?

How has that person left a lasting impact on you?

5) If you could choose a lesson to be left behind for someone, what would that lesson be?

How can you go about leaving that lesson?

6) If someone could walk a mile in your shoes, where would you want that mile to be?

From what season of your life would that mile have been walked?

The twins

George and Dave Kullgren

An afternoon gathering in Sweden

Opposite page: Pop's choir in New York City

Pop and Jenn Kullgren McCaughan

Memories of Pop from the Family

"Most of all, Grandpa, I cherish the memories from my wedding. The photo shoot we did before the big day. Seeing you all dressed up in a tux and getting to dance with you. These are just a few of my fondest memories and I can't wait to share more with you. You are one in a million!!!"

Jenn Kullgren McCaughan

"When Pop left Sweden, he took with him many memories of his family he had left behind, but also of changes that were soon to take place in his life. Now, those memories are still tucked away and as fresh as the day he left Sweden. His family here in the United States is close with the family he left behind.

Pop brought with him a loving heart, a fondness for music, a belief in Christ, and a strong work ethic. He has been able to mold lives with both his warm heart and his wonderful large hand. With a gentle touch, he shaped not only the wood products he worked with his hands, but also our minds.

On Sunday mornings, you will find him sitting in the third pew on the right side singing songs to his heart's content. From my view in the choir, I get to watch the expressions on his face as familiar tunes are played and sung. What a wonderful sight to behold!"

Dave Kullgren

"Pop owned a black car with running boards in the 1940's. When he came home from work, he would pause a moment at the end of the driveway. Dave and I would "jump on the running boards and hold on to the door handles" as Pop drove the rest of the way to the garage.

Buying a "new car" was different in the "old days." You did not use the Internet or go to a car dealer. In our neighborhood, a car salesman would drive by in a car and ask if you wanted to test drive the car. One Saturday he stopped and talked to Pop about getting a new car. We watched and waited. Pop said "yes" and later we had a "new" used car.

When we were growing up, Sunday was different. We went to two or three different church services. Pop always sang in the church choir. When we were young, we would always stay in our Sunday clothes all day. After church, the family - combined families - would have lunch together, then go for long walks...in our Sunday clothes. Although the years have come and gone, church is still the focal point of Pop's life."

George Kullgren

"The thing that impresses me most about Grandpa are his hands. When I was young, I was always fascinated with his hands. The real fascination was with the strength of his grip. Every year my family would visit for the Holidays and all of the grandkids would line up to shake his hand. We would all squeeze as hard as we could for 10 seconds while Grandpa would stand there smiling. He would then start to squeeze back until all of us were on our knees screaming, 'Mercy!'

I'm pretty sure that he could still make me cry mercy even today."

Jonathan Kullgren

"My earliest memories of Grandpa include visiting him in Florida, where he instructed me on the proper techniques for catching geckos. Later, I remember every year planning my strategy for shaking his hand. I could never figure out how to get the stronger grip. Every year, the results were the same. He was smiling and I was usually on my knees asking to be released from his grip.

At any family gathering, I can remember his inspections of my father's and Uncle Dave's carpentry. Invariably the words "wood butchers" would find their way into the conversation.

My favorite story is when Grandpa came to visit on a day the contractors were applying grass seed to the yard of our new house in Maryland. Of course they were not doing their job correctly - in fact, they were doing fairly shoddy work. I imagine as he looked across the rock-strewn lot, he could envision the lawn, or lack thereof, in a year's time. He grabbed a rake and proceeded to rake all of the stones out of the yard before they could seed. This story captures the essence of his character - "do the job right the first time."

Christopher Kullgren

This Is My Song
A Musical Journey Through the Life of Harry "Pop" Kullgren

Companion Musical CD for *Be Still, My Soul*
featuring Jamie Purser, Catherine Ritch Guess and
Harry "Pop" Kullgren

ISBN: 1-933341-12-2;   (13-digit)978-1-933341-12-5
$15.95

This Is My Song

A Musical Journey Through the Life of Harry "Pop" Kullgren

Companion Musical CD for *Be Still, My Soul*

ISBN: 1-933341-12-2;   (13-digit)978-1-933341-12-5

Original Arrangements by
Catherine Ritch Guess and Jamie Purser,
recorded with "Pop" Kullgren include:

Be Still, My Soul
Blott en dag
To Everything There Is a Season
Leaning on the Everlasting Arms
This Is My Song
America, the Beautiful
Bless This House
Dwelling In Beulah Land
How Great Thou Art
Were You There
Free at Last
The Lord's Prayer
and
*Conversation with Pop and Catherine
at the recording session*

Need a Conference Idea or Speaker?

Catherine Ritch Guess, in addition to her writing, is a frequent speaker and musician for a variety of conferences, retreats and seminars throughout the US. She and her son, Jamie Purser, regularly do concerts and events to go with each of her book series. After working as an Organist/Minister of Music for nearly 35 years, Catherine sees this as an answer to her prayer that God would use her outside the "four walls of the church."

With *Be Still, My Soul*, Catherine has developed a program - for one or several sessions - that is ideal for groups who fall in the spring, the summer, the autumn or the winter seasons of their lives. She has also tailored this program to work with people of all seasons within the same group.

For more information on this, or any other of Catherine's specially-designed programs, or for questions regarding a specific focus for your group, you may contact CRM BOOKS - crm@ciridmus.com

If you would like to schedule Catherine Ritch Guess, and/or Jamie Purser, for your next concert or event, you may reach them at crguess@ciridmus.com

www.catherineritchguess.com

Other Titles by Catherine Ritch Guess

EAGLE'S WINGS TRILOGY
Love Lifted Me
Higher Ground

SHOOTING STAR SERIES
In the Bleak Midwinter
A Song in the Air

SANDMAN SERIES
Old Rugged Cross
Let Us Break Bread Together

Musical Sculptures
A CD of Original Compositions and Arrangements
by Catherine Ritch Guess

LIFT UP MINE EYES SERIES
Tis So Sweet

STAND ALONE TITLES
In the Garden
Church in the Wildwood
For the Beauty of the Earth

FOR CHILDREN:
WHITE SQUIRREL PARABLES
Kipper Finds a Home

Upcoming Titles by Catherine Ritch Guess

Victory in Jesus
3rd Volume of the Sandman Series

Rudy, the Red Pig
A New Children's Series

In the Sweet By and By
The 1st Volume of
"The Winsome Ways of Miz Eudora Rumph"

The Friendly Beasts
A Sandman Christmas Story

The Midnight Clear
3rd Volume of the Shooting Star Series

Rudy's Magic Sleigh
Children's Christmas Book

Zipper Finds a Job
A White Squirrel Parable

This Is My Song

A Musical Journey Through the Life of
Harry "Pop" Kullgren

Featuring
Jamie Purser
Catherine Ritch Guess
Harry Kullgren

This Is My Song
Companion Musical CD for *Be Still, My Soul*

This Is My Song represents the young, the middle-aged and the elderly in such a stirring blend that it is sure to touch the heart of every American. *And Swede!* From the dignity of *Bless This House* and *The Lord's Prayer* to the "campy" revivals styles of *Leaning on the Everlasting Arms* and *Dwelling in Beulah Land*, *This Is My Song* is a beautiful sharing of a man in the "winter" of his life's journey that undisputedly shows that *everyone*, no matter how young or old, has a wondrous gift to share, and that we truly *are* "One Nation Under God," as his singing of *America, the Beautiful* depicts.